100 BEAUTIFUL VIEWS OF GLACIER NATIONAL PARK

Roy E. Hughes

HAPPY TRAILS!
ROY

WESTCLIFFE PUBLISHERS

www.bigearthpublishing.com

International Standard Book Number: 978-1-56579-632-4
Text and Art: © 2009 by Roy E. Hughes. All rights reserved.
www.royehughes.com

Editor: Ali Geiser
Cover and text design: Rebecca Finkel

Published by:
Westcliffe Publishers,
a Big Earth Publishing company
1637 Pearl Street, Suite 201
Boulder, Colorado 80302

Printed in Canada by Friesens

9 8 7 6 5 4 3 2 1

Library of Congress Cataloging-in-Publication Data:

Hughes, Roy E.
100 beautiful views of Glacier National Park / Roy E. Hughes.
p. cm.
ISBN 978-1-56579-632-4
1. Hughes, Roy E. 2. Glacier National Park (Mont.)—In art.
I. Title. II. Title: One hundred beautiful views of Glacier National Park.

NE539.H83A4 2009
917.86'52—dc22
2008047961

For more information about other fine books and calendars from
Westcliffe Publishers, a Big Earth Publishing company,
please contact your local bookstore, call us at 1-800-258-5830,
or visit us on the Web at bigearthpublishing.com.

To view this and more artwork online, visit www.royhughes.com.

Cover art: St. Mary Lake Jammer
Title page art: Granite Park Chalet
Opposite: Fireweed

PLEASE NOTE: The author and publisher of this book have made
every effort to ensure the accuracy and currency of its information.
Nevertheless, books can require revisions. Please feel free to let us know
if you find information in this book that needs to be updated,
and we will be glad to correct it for the next printing.
Your comments and suggestions are always welcome.

To all those who strive

to preserve the grand beauty of

Glacier National Park.

Contents

I AM A MONTANA NATIVE SON, having been born in Hamilton in the Bitterroot Valley. My stay there was short lived, however. Two weeks after I was born, my mother took me to live in Spokane where my father had gone to take a job as a mechanic. Although I left Montana as a home, I never left it in spirit, and I continue to return to the state time and time again.

In 1914, my mother's parents had moved from Czechoslovakia to a farm on Grave Creek, near Fortine. The farm, or "The Ranch" as we called it, was a favorite place for our family to retreat to. My father would often return from work on a Friday afternoon and say, "Let's go to The Ranch." We would hurriedly pack the car and head off into the darkening evening, arriving near midnight to be welcomed by abruptly awakened grandparents and Uncle Chuck.

During my childhood years, The Ranch became my home away from home. We visited there weekends and sometimes for a week or more during the summers, often to help with the haying. At the young age of eight or nine, I was not aware of Glacier National Park or its beauty and allure, but the area around the ranch was comprised of the same beauty—In fact, The Ranch was only about 30 miles west of the border of the park.

The fond memories of those childhood times at the ranch were so strong that I later wrote of them in a graduate writing class. I think that the resultant piece captures my sentiments regarding that part of Montana.

Forests rested at the base of tall mountains as the shadow of night crept up the steep slopes bidding the nodding trees goodnight.

I recall the frequent summer trips which began fifty and more years ago from our house in Spokane to this place where my mother was raised. I remember my field-tilling grandparents, immigrants from Czechoslovakia, via a Van Gogh drawing. Babba and Dédek, Grandma and Grandpa. And Chuck, younger then, the handsome bachelor.

The late summer evenings I remember most when, stomachs filled with puffy dinner dumplings, my smaller sister and I begged pushes on the tall swing beneath the purpled and closer sky. Warm-hued air stirred by on its way up the mountains to cool and sleep for the night. Forests rested at the base of tall mountains as the shadow of night crept up the steep slopes bidding the nodding trees goodnight.

Then Dédek, Grandpa, appeared with his magical accordion hanging bulkily from his slight and weathered frame. Strains of delicious music floated forth filling the diminishing world with songs from another land and another time. Grandma and Mom and Chuck would be caught, at times, pacing the melody with gently nodding heads and almost imperceptible hums.

As darkness finally closed the door on day, the pastel glow of a kerosene lamp found its way to an unlighted window signaling the concert's end. We would move inside to the beckoning light, leaving the big dipper and maybe the aurora to guard the sky 'til morning.

After my grandparents died, my uncle, Chuck, took over the ranch. As he grew older, I would often visit him just after the Fourth of July to help with the haying. Chuck always enjoyed "taking a drive" when there was a break in the work, and his favorite drive was up Grave Creek toward Therriault Pass, then over "the hump" on an almost non-existent road, dropping down to the North Fork of the Flathead River road, stopping for lunch at Polebridge, then completing a loop south to Columbia Falls, west to Whitefish, then north back to Grave Creek.

The bone-jarring drive was gloriously scenic and populated with wild animals ranging from deer and moose to grizzly bears and mountain lions.

This bone-jarring drive was gloriously scenic and populated with wild animals ranging from deer and moose to grizzly bears and mountain lions. As we neared the North Fork, the crenellated mountain tops of northern Glacier National Park would begin to appear on the eastern horizon. The drive south along the North Fork allowed us spectacular views into the mountains in the Kintla Lake area.

At times we would enter the park "through the back door" at Polebridge and explore its less-traveled northwest areas, from Kintla Lake on the north to Bowman Lake, then bounce down the rough inside road to Lake McDonald for the reward of a huckleberry ice cream cone. Or we would bypass the rugged inside road and take the less-rough North Fork Road and enter the park at the Camas Creek entrance. The impressions that these back-door explorations of the park made on me were strong and remained with me, drawing me back again and again.

My Art Background

In college I studied art and eventually became a teacher of art in the public schools. But as time passed, I drifted away from art as I became involved in the emerging field of computer technology in education. I gravitated to computer graphics, applying my art training in that area and teaching at the community college level.

After I had semi-retired, I took a refresher watercolor class. I began painting watercolors in earnest, using our farm animals as subjects: chickens, sheep, horses, llamas, dogs, and cats. Encouraged by being accepted into juried shows and winning a prize along the way, I expanded my painting horizons by taking some oil painting classes. I enjoyed painting oil landscapes, especially mountains, and attributed this affinity to my love of hiking in the North Cascades of Washington State.

I don't know whether I am a hiker who paints or a painter who hikes.

I don't know whether I am a hiker who paints or a painter who hikes. Nonetheless, I found myself creating a series of oil paintings of the areas in which I hiked in the North Cascades. Although I tried plein air painting in the mountains, I found lugging the extra painting gear and trying to capture the rapidly changing light unrewarding. However, knowing that I would paint a scene or more from each hike made me more aware and observant of my surroundings. And I discovered that this added awareness, combined with the hundred or more digital photos I'd take per hike, allowed me to create the type of paintings that I desired.

Being a student of art, I have explored many artists and techniques. I am drawn to the ukiyo-e, or wood block printing, of Japanese artists such as Hiroshige and Hokusai. I admire the beautiful landscape compositions and the use of color in these prints. Perhaps the study of this technique is what drew me to appreciate the wood block print and silkscreen posters done in the 1920s and '30s by such artists as Maurice Logan and Norman Fraser. These two styles of art led me to investigate the possibility of creating images that looked similar to wood block and silkscreen prints using the computer. The artwork you see in this book is the result.

Digital Block Prints

Digital block prints look much like wood block and silkscreen prints. The signature of this medium is large, flat areas of bold color that create a poster-like effect. The process of creating this type of art can be imagined as painting each color seen in an image on a transparent piece of glass, then stacking each color layer on top of the preceding layer until all of the layers are completed.

Sometimes I will end up with nearly two hundred layers in an image.

Wood block prints and silk screens usually require one block or screen per color. Each block or screen is prepared and printed in a particular order, with each new color layer registered so that the colors of one layer are aligned properly with the color edges of other layers. Complex scenes may require over a hundred blocks or screens, making the process quite labor intensive.

A computer makes this process much more manageable. Using Adobe Photoshop, a graphics editing program, I begin with a reference photograph, then create layers of color on top of the photograph until I have created a layer for each color used in the image. I generally begin with the area of the image that appears farthest back—say the sky in a landscape—and create the first layer of color for that. If the sky contains clouds, there will be one or more layers created for the clouds, depending on how may colors I interpret in the clouds. Sometimes I will end up with nearly two hundred layers in an image. The completed image is then digitally "flattened," or merged into one single image, before being printed out.

The Glacier National Park Artist-in-Residence Program

A number of national parks in the United States have artist-in-residence programs. The program in Glacier has been in existence since 1998. Since that time approximately forty artists have served residencies. Many of these artists have been painters or photographers, however, the program is open to writers, filmmakers, and other types of artists as well. In 2005, I was one of two artists selected for a four-week residency. During this time, I was provided a cabin on the shores of Lake McDonald and charged with "doing art." In return, I donated one piece of completed art to the park and conducted several informal presentations and one formal talk per week to educate the public about the artist-in-residence program. The work that follows was created from this experience.

x

Introduction

GLACIER NATIONAL PARK sits astride the Continental Divide in northwestern Montana. It borders Waterton Lakes National Park in Canada, and in 1932 the two were designated as the Waterton-Glacier International Peace Park—a symbol of peace and friendship between the U.S. and Canada and the world's first International Peace Park. This unified park—the inspiration for this book— is a part of an ecosystem that has become known as "the Crown of the Continent." At a million-plus acres, the park is a bit larger in size than the state of Rhode Island.

In 2007, the park attracted over two million visitors who came to drink in the beauty of the scenery and hope for a glimpse of the many types of wild animals in the area. There are a number of distinct geographical areas in the park. This book is divided according to these areas—each of which has influenced me in their own way.

Although I have visited the park many times, the impressions recorded in the artwork here are based on my month-long experience as artist-in-residence during July and August of 2005. Most of these images were originally created to be what I call "small posters" (13 inches tall by 9.5 inches wide), maintaining the format of old travel posters used by the Great Northern Railway to entice travelers from the east to come to Glacier in the park's early years. The railway was a driving force in the creation of the park. Their strategy was to create a "destination" for rail travelers by building hotels and providing tourist services, thus expanding their profits beyond ticket sales.

After creating a great number of the small posters, I decided to try a panorama format to see if I could capture the feel of the bigness of Glacier. These panoramas are 10 inches tall and however wide it takes to capture the scene. They are printed on canvas and framed with a black "floater" frame. Some of these panoramas run 40 inches wide or more.

CHAPTER 1. Going-to-the-Sun Corridor

The Going-to-the-Sun corridor is the most visited area of the park. For many people, going to Glacier National Park is synonymous with driving Going-to-the-Sun Road. The Works Project Administration constructed this winding, scenic, 50-mile byway during the Great Depression. The road winds its way from the hamlet of St. Mary at the east entrance to the park up and over Logan Pass and descends via twisty switchbacks to Lake McDonald and past Apgar, eventually reaching the park entrance at West Glacier.

Going-to-the-Sun Road officially opened on July 15, 1933. Actual work began on the road in 1921. The road was constructed from both the east side and the west side, with the two sections meeting at Logan Pass.

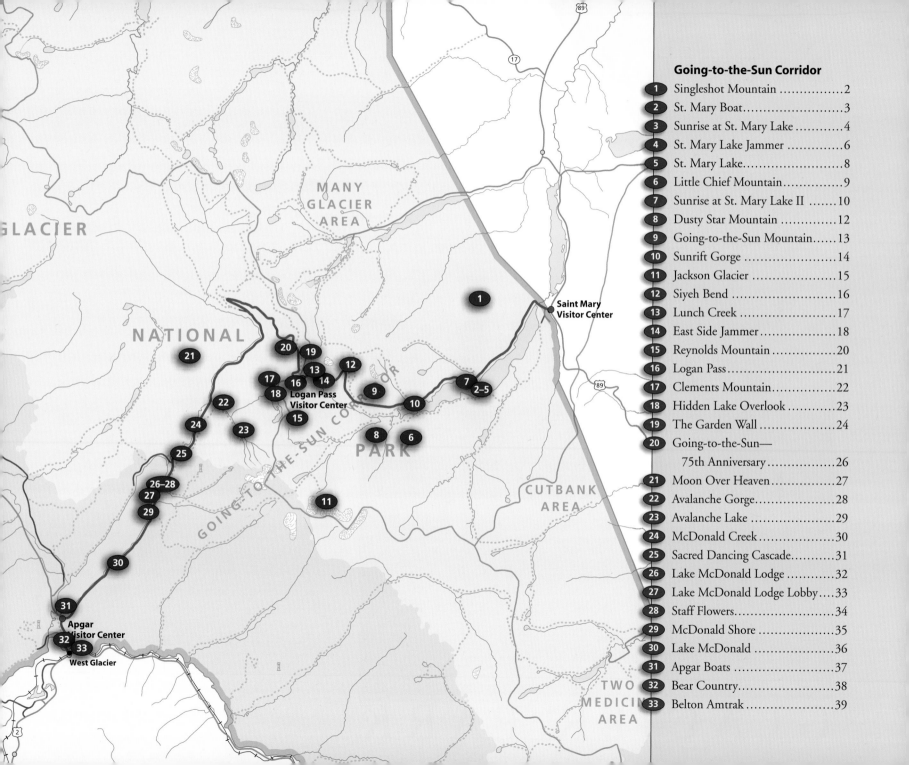

Going-to-the-Sun Corridor

Singleshot Mountain

GLACIER PARK

1 *Singleshot Mountain* is located near the east entrance to Glacier National Park at St. Mary. The long mountain runs west to east alongside the Going-to-the-Sun Road. It gets its name from the story that George Bird Grinnell, hunting in this area before Glacier was a national park, killed a mountain goat with only one long, accurate shot.

Grinnell was an early explorer of the area and perhaps the most instrumental person in encouraging the government to set aside the land for a national park. A number of places in the park are named after him, including Grinnell Glacier and Grinnell Lake, both in the Many Glacier area.

This scene shows the sun shining over the mountains to the east of the park at dawn. Travelers arriving at sunrise on a clear day can watch the early morning clouds burn off and golden shafts of light strike Singleshot Mountain obliquely, turning the entire mountain into a huge gold nugget.

② *St. Mary Boat:* Glacier Park Scenic Boat Tours offer boat rides on St. Mary Lake as well as other lakes in the park. This dock is located about 6.5 miles west of St. Mary, near the Rising Sun Motor Inn and Campground on the south side of Going-to-the-Sun Road.

The name of this boat is *Little Chief.* It is one of several boats built by J.W. Swanson in 1925. This boat cruises the lake, passing such places as Wild Goose Island and Baring Falls.

During a cruise the boat captain describes the flora, fauna, geology, and history of this region of the park. In addition to viewing the tremendous scenery around the lake, it is often possible to view wildlife. Daily during the summer, a ranger-led hike to St. Mary Falls is combined with the boat cruise.

St Mary Boat

© 2005 Roy E Hughes - www.royehughes.com

GLACIER PARK

4

3 *Sunrise at St. Mary Lake:* This view looks east, back toward St. Mary, from several miles up the lake on Going-to-the-Sun Road. The sun is just breaking over the eastern hills and reflecting on St. Mary Lake. The panoramas in Glacier Park are stunning and change in appearance depending on the weather, the time of day, and the season of the year.

④ *St. Mary Lake Jammer:* When you're driving west along St. Mary Lake in the early morning, the sun obliquely illuminates the golden slope to the north, while the mountains to the south are still hidden in shadows. It's an awesome sight.

The vehicle in this image is one of the fleet of red buses that ply the park. They were built and used in the mid-twentieth century, fell into poor condition, and were rebuilt by the Ford Motor Company over an 18-month period beginning in 2000. Ford donated the cost of the restoration.

These red buses are a favorite of visitors to Glacier. They are often referred to as "jammers," although their drivers object to this terminology as they refer to themselves as the jammers. The term evolved in the old days when recalcitrant gearshifts often had to be jammed into place. Some drivers become a bit testy if you point out that the term jammer is now obsolete since the refurbished buses have automatic transmissions that don't need to be manually shifted.

St Mary Lake

© 2005 Roy E Hughes · www.royehughes.com

GLACIER PARK

5 *St. Mary Lake* stretches for 10 miles, from the eastern St. Mary park entrance west through a glacier-gouged valley along the south side of Going-to-the-Sun Road. Rugged mountains line both sides of the lake: Singleshot Mountain, Going-to-the-Sun Mountain, and Matahpi Peak on the north and Little Chief, Dusty Star, and other mountains on the south.

There is a very small island in the lake named Wild Goose Island. The view in this image is from the Wild Goose Island Turnout, about 7 miles west of the St. Mary entrance. This is a very popular location from which to take photographs of St. Mary Lake—and a favorite place for weddings. This is the view looking west, up the valley toward Logan Pass.

Actually, there are two St. Mary Lakes: Upper St. Mary Lake, usually called simply St. Mary Lake, and Lower St. Mary Lake, which lies north of the townlet of St. Mary outside the east entrance to the park. The St. Mary River connects the two lakes.

6 *Little Chief Mountain* looms over the south side of St. Mary Lake and can be seen in the distance in the previous two views. It rises to an elevation of 9,541 feet. People do climb it; the ascent involves over 5,000 feet of elevation gain and is rated as Class 3, indicating steep scrambling and moderate exposure. Little Chief is a popular name. The boat on St. Mary Lake carries it, as did a Great Northern Railway observation car.

Little Chief

GLACIER PARK

7 *Sunrise at St. Mary Lake 2:* Even in summer, predawn early mornings are chilly at this location. However, folks often brave the shadowed morning chill to watch the sun rise and light the lake and valley.

In this scene the north side of the lake is bathed in a golden glow while the mountains to the south are still swathed in darkness. A full moon hangs in the dawn. The lighting effect is peaceful yet stunning. Except for the presence of the Going-to-the-Sun Road, this scene is much like one that George Bird Grinnell, who is considered by many to be the father of Glacier Park, would have seen when he first viewed the lake in 1885.

Dusty Star

© 2005 Roy E Hughes - www.royehughes.com

GLACIER PARK

8 *Dusty Star Mountain* is just west of Little Chief Mountain. Just the name makes one curious about this place. The Glacier National Park name authority, Jack Holterman, provides two possible explanations for it in his book *Place Names of Glacier/Waterton National Parks.* First, American Indians passing over or toward this mountain often saw meteors. Their term for meteor translates as "dusty star." A second explanation focuses on a type of mushroom found on the flanks of the mountain. The mushrooms are called dusty stars. Take your choice.

This huge chunk of rock is imposing, reminding some of the huge monolith Chief Mountain in the Belly River area of the northeast corner of the park. The stark stone pillar rises from verdant forests, providing a wonderful contrast in shape, textures, and color.

Dusty Star Mountain is fantastically popular with photographers. My reference photo did not clearly show all the characteristics of the mountain that I wanted for this view, so I searched for images of it on the Internet until I found a shot with the qualities I was looking for. I contacted the photographer and got his permission to use his image as a reference photo in return for a print of the finished artwork. This was a win-win situation.

9 *Going-to-the-Sun Mountain* is over 9,600 feet tall. This view of the mountain is from Sun Point, a peninsula that juts into St. Mary Lake about 10 miles east of the park entrance. Trails beginning at Sun Point wrap around the peninsula, offering grand views of the lake both to the east and to the west.

Going-to-the-Sun Mountain has a famous name, the origin of which is in doubt. An early area explorer, James Willard Schultz, claims to have named the peak. However, there is also a Blackfeet legend that involves a vision quest to the mountain. The Blackfeet name for the mountain translates as "to the sun he goes," Or, more comprehensively, "The-Face-of-Sour-Spirit-Who-Went-Back-to-The-Sun-After-His-Work-Was-Done Mountain." And you thought Going-to-the-Sun Mountain was a mouthful.

Wreathed by a wisp of pearlescent cloud, the luminescent mountain looks rather magical, giving credence to the Blackfeet legend that it is a sacred place. If you are fortunate in your travels, you may arrive here in lighting and weather conditions that bathe the scene in a sacred light.

Going-to-the-Sun Mountain

© 2005 Roy E Hughes - www.royehughes.com

GLACIER PARK

10 *Sunrift Gorge,* located about 10.5 miles west of St. Mary, is easy to drive by. The bridge over the gorge conceals its beauty, and a driver can cross it and pass on by without knowing.

To see the gorge proper, most people head upstream from the road, hiking north on the Siyeh Pass trail. However, the path winding beneath the bridge to the south side of the road leads to this beautiful scene. Follow a trail south toward St. Mary Lake to reach Baring Falls, another popular photography subject.

11 *Jackson Glacier* turnout is a little over 13 miles from the St. Mary entrance to the park, on the south side of Going-to-the-Sun Road. Although the turnout and exhibit are marked by signs, they are easy to miss, not only because Jackson Glacier lies far to the south of the road, but because Jackson Glacier is no longer as impressive as it once was.

At one time, Jackson Glacier was part of Blackfoot Glacier and several other glaciers that extended across the Continental Divide. Jackson Glacier split off sometime before 1929. There is evidence that all glaciers in Glacier National Park are shrinking, and that in a couple of generations there will be none left within the park. Support for this derives from the United States Geologic Survey Repeat Photography Project where current photos of the park's glaciers are compared to archived photos of the same scene taken in the early 1900s.

Jackson Glacier

© 2005 Roy E Hughes - www.royehughes.com

GLACIER PARK

Siyeh Bend

GLACIER PARK

© 2005 Roy E Hughes · www.royehughes.com

12 *Siyeh Bend* is a sweeping curve on the Going-to-the-Sun Road about 15.5 miles from the east entrance. From here, you can look up the Siyeh Valley to see 10,000-plus-foot Mount Siyeh looming above. This mountain looks unusual in that it doesn't have the rugged, rocky confirmation often found in the tectonically buckled stone of the park. Its Blackfeet name translates into "rabid wolf" or "rabid dog."

Energetic hikers can climb over 2,000 feet in about 5 miles to reach Siyeh Pass, passing along the shoulder of Going-to-the-Sun Mountain. Even more energetic hikers can undertake a 10-mile hike, descending the Baring Creek drainage to Sunrift Gorge. Less energetic travelers can enjoy this view from the road.

13 *Lunch Creek* was named after what was eaten there. Tour groups often stopped at this scenic bend about 17 miles west of St. Mary. This is the view looking north up the creek toward Mount Piegan, looming square-topped on the ridge. There are no approved hiking trails that head up this drainage. So many "unofficial" trails have been made by visitors stopping at the bend and walking along the creek that a restoration project had to be undertaken a few years ago to replant much of the area near the road.

Lunch Creek

GLACIER PARK

14 *East Side Jammer:* There are two tunnels on the Going-to-the-Sun Road, one on the west side of Logan Pass and this one—the East Side Tunnel—on the east side, about 17 miles from St. Mary. When the Going-to-the-Sun Road was being constructed in the 1920s and '30s, this 405-foot-long tunnel proved quite a challenge. No heavy equipment could reach the site, and all of the excavation had to be done by hand, with workers carting all the rock from the tunnel. The tunnel is listed on the Historic American Engineering Record as a unique entity due to the fact that its construction relied heavily upon hand labor. I wonder if the folks who honk their horns while passing through the tunnel are celebrating this accomplishment.

Reynolds Mountain
Half Summer ~ Half Winter

© 2005 Roy E Hughes - www.royehughes.com

GLACIER PARK

15 *Reynolds Mountain* is a Matterhorn-shaped peak near Logan Pass. There are several different routes of varying degrees of difficulty that lead to its summit. The views from the top are spectacular.

I often get Reynolds and Clements Mountains mixed up, as they look similar. Clements Mountain is seen looming to the west of the visitor center at Logan Pass, while Reynolds Mountain is to the south.

So, what's with the snow on half the mountain? Since Going-to-the-Sun Road is closed in the winter, most people see the mountain only in summer. I thought that it would be interesting for people to see what the mountain looked like in winter.

16 *Logan Pass* tops Going-to-the-Sun Road at the Continental Divide at an elevation of 6,646 feet. The pass is 18 miles from St. Mary and about 32 miles from the West Glacier park entrance.

During the height of tourist season, it is best to arrive at the pass before 10:00 a.m., or parking may be non-existent. This is a "must-stop" spot on the itinerary of the Red Buses, tour groups, and every tourist driving Going-to-the-Sun Road. The visitors' center and restrooms are a welcome sight after winding upward to the pass.

The views from the pass are splendid in any direction. The air is fresh and cool. In July wild-flowers carpet the area with a rainbow of color. Mountain goats can often be seen wandering the alpine meadows.

Many walks and hikes radiate from Logan Pass, allowing adventurers to roam on the board-walk trail to Hidden Lake Overlook or to head north along the Highline Trail. Clements Mountain rises to the west beyond the visitor center.

Logan Pass

GLACIER PARK

© 2005 Roy E Hughes - www.royehughes.com

Clements Mountain

GLACIER PARK

17 *Clements Mountain* is viewed here from the Going-to-the-Sun Road. If you look closely you can see the road cut in the upper right-hand corner of the image, where it approaches Logan Pass. The cliffs in the mid-ground are the end of a hanging valley where a glacier once terminated. There are many such valleys in the park.

If you stop at the Two Dog Flats Restaurant, about 6 miles west of St. Mary, you will see a large oil painting by John Fery, an early painter for the Great Northern Railway. Although his scene is a panorama, the view is similar to the one in this depiction. For a wonderful book about early artists of the park, from painters to photographers to sculptors, read Larry Len Peterson's *The Call of the Mountains: The Artists of Glacier National Park.*

18 *Hidden Lake Overlook:* Want to take a civilized hike, a fair amount of which is on pavement or boardwalk? Hidden Lake Overlook is the trail for you. The walk begins behind the Logan Pass Visitor Center, climbing uphill on a boardwalk with spectacular mountain views on all sides. In late July the area is resplendent with wildflowers. Mountain goats frequent this area and are accustomed enough to people that they may lay down on the trail or browse contentedly close to the byway.

At 3 miles roundtrip and with less than 500 feet elevation gain, the hike is short and scenic. This trail is so heavily trafficked that a good part of it, where it does not cross rock areas, is boardwalk and pavement to protect the fragile meadow areas.

One and a half miles along the trail is the overlook platform, which provides a wide-angle view of Hidden Lake below and the mountains beyond. Adventurous souls may continue on to the lake, a descent of nearly 800 feet that must be regained on the hike out. Be aware that the area around Hidden Lake is often closed due to bear activity. Signs at the trailheads alert hikers to these situations and it is unwise and illegal to ignore these warnings.

Hidden Lake Overlook

GLACIER PARK

© 2005 Roy E Hughes - www.royehughes.com

19 *The Garden Wall:* Just west of the summit of Logan Pass there is a pullout and a viewing platform that allows westbound visitors the first views of McDonald Valley and the ridge of the Continental Divide as it sweeps north. In the 1890s the jagged section of the divide just north of Logan Pass was named The Garden Wall after the song "Over the Garden Wall," which was popular at the time.

This view has so much going on in it. Most dramatic is the ridge of the Continental Divide. Additionally, you can follow the rise of Going-to-the-Sun Road from the valley floor. And if you know where to look, you can see the Highline Trail as it traverses the mountainside between the road and the ridgeline. The Highline Trail, which winds north from Logan Pass to Granite Park Chalet and beyond, is a favorite place of many hikers. You'll learn more about this marvelous place in chapter six.

Going-to-the-Sun
75th Anniversary

© 2008 Roy Hughes - www.royhughes.com

GLACIER PARK

20 *Going-to-the-Sun—75th Anniversary:* This view of the Going-to-the-Sun Road is on the steep west side approach to Logan Pass at a point called Triple Arches. This section of the 50-mile road was the most difficult to build, as it rises about 3,000 feet in the last 9 miles before reaching Logan Pass. The terrain is steep and cliff-like, and much blasting away of the hillside was necessary to gouge the road out of the mountains.

The roadway is paved and walls or guardrails line the outside edge, however, the outside of the drop is precipitous and seems exaggerated when you're rounding the left-hand hairpin turns along the route. Motor homes and vehicles towing trailers are banned from this road because of the narrow width and steep grades. For those who don't want to drive themselves, red buses and shuttle vans are available.

21 *Moon Over Heaven:* Heaven's Peak— what a name, what a place. About halfway along Going-to-the-Sun Road, a few miles west of Logan Pass, is this stunning view of Heaven's Peak across McDonald Valley to the north.

Although the name Heaven's Peak came from a white prospector, it matches the Blackfeet name, which translates roughly as "where God lives."

This peak is viewable from many points in the park and is gorgeous from any angle and in any light. In the pre-dawn light shown here, the mountain does indeed look heavenly. The scene begs for a moon and artistic license allows me to supply it.

In 1943 a stone fire lookout was built atop this mountain, but it was not used much and has since been abandoned. For those who are interested, there are a couple of routes to the top of the mountain.

Moon Over Heaven

GLACIER PARK

Avalanche Gorge

© 2005 Roy E Hughes • www.royehughes.com

GLACIER PARK

22 *Avalanche Gorge:* The Avalanche Campground area, 34 miles from St. Mary and 16 miles from West Glacier, is the first major attraction after descending the west side of Logan Pass. A short hike on boardwalk along the Trail of the Cedars is an attraction for those who don't want to stray too far from their cars, or those in wheelchairs. Avalanche Gorge is situated at the far point of the loop, less than 1 mile from the parking areas. Thomas Schmidt, in *Glacier and Waterton Lakes National Parks Road Guide,* describes the gorge as "Where an achingly beautiful stretch of sapphire water swirls over rock nearly blood red." For the more adventurous, at the far point of the Cedars loop a trail leads upward to Avalanche Gorge and beyond to Avalanche Lake, depicted in the next view.

23 *Avalanche Lake* is really not "on" the Going-to-the-Sun Road, but the Avalanche Lake camping area and trailhead are. Follow the Trail of the Cedars to reach Avalanche Gorge, where the short and extremely popular trail to Avalanche Lake begins.

This forested hike is only 4 miles long round-trip and has less than 500 feet of elevation gain. Late July is usually not the optimum time to view Avalanche Lake from an aesthetic point of view, as the lake level is low and you can see the muddy bottom extending far into the lake. However, there were still several waterfalls dropping a pleasant amount of water off the cliffs beyond the lake when I captured this view.

Avalanche Lake

GLACIER PARK

McDonald Creek

© 2005 Roy E Hughes · www.royehughes.com

GLACIER PARK

24 *McDonald Creek* originates near Mount Gedhun. It approaches the Going-to-the-Sun Road near The Loop on the road's descent from Logan Pass. The best view of McDonald Creek is found between Avalanche Campground and the north end of Lake McDonald. This view is from that location, an observation platform accessed from one of the several viewing turnouts on Going-to-the-Sun Road. Here the creek has cut through its bedrock over the years, creating a narrow channel through which the water rushes.

On sunny summer afternoons, the shadows cast by the south bank of the creek and the rushing sound of the water provide a cooling effect to an otherwise hot setting. One wonders if the creek looked the same on an August afternoon in 1890 when Lieutenant George Ahern and his party, the first Europeans to explore the area, visited here on an exploration of the mountains north of Marias Pass.

Sacred Dancing Cascade

25 *Sacred Dancing Cascade* on McDonald Creek is located between the previous McDonald Creek image site and the north end of Lake McDonald. The cascade's lovely name once applied to several locations in the Lake McDonald Valley. Sacred Dancing is a translation of a Kootenai, or Kutenais, Indian term meaning, loosely, "a good place to dance." The Kootenai applied the same name to Lake McDonald, according to naturalist George Ruhle, who writes that the American Indians came to this area during the summer to perform ceremonial rites. Ruhle attempted, over the years, to have several names in this area changed back to Sacred Dancing, but only to this stretch of water was the old name restored.

© 2005 Roy E Hughes - www.royehughes.com

GLACIER PARK

© 2005 Roy E Hughes - www.royehughes.com

26 *Lake McDonald Lodge* is 40 miles from St. Mary and 10 from West Glacier at Snyder Creek. There is a restaurant here and a country store and even a small post office. The centerpiece of the complex is the lodge.

Before the park was a park, there was a hotel located here. The Great Northern Railway finally bought out the owner and created the lodge. The history of the hotel and lodge are very interesting. To find out more, read *View with a Room* by Ray Djuff and Chris Morrison.

This view is actually of the back of the lodge. The building's imposing front facade faces Lake McDonald. At one time you could look up from the lake and see the lodge boldly sitting atop its knoll, but today trees have grown up between the shore and the building, obscuring the view of the building from the lake and of the lake from the building.

Although this view is not particularly aesthetic, it captures the hustle and bustle that is always going on around the lodge. The lodge is a meeting place as well as a point of departure for red bus tours heading to the east side of the park.

27 *Lake McDonald Lodge Lobby:*
Ah, comfort and class—that's what the interiors of the park's hotels convey. The Lake McDonald Lodge lobby is not as grand and massive as those of Many Glacier Hotel and Glacier Park Lodge in East Glacier, but it is cozier.

This is a view looking from the west side of the lobby toward the registration desk. To the right, out of view, is a monster of a fireplace, one that you can stand up and spread your arms in and not touch the sides. Most of the time, often even in summer, there is a roaring fire going there.

The decor of the lobby is "old west" style—rustic timbers, American Indian motifs on the lampshades, stuffed animals, and old paintings—but it strikes me as art deco as well. That's the feel that I get from this view.

Much more lodge lies outside the scene. There is a gift shop, the Charlie Russell dining room, and a cozy bar where one can get a burger and local microbrew and leisurely lunch while looking out at the lake and mountains beyond. This is a splendid place.

Lake McDonald Lodge Lobby

© 2006 Roy E. Hughes - www.royehughes.com

GLACIER PARK

Staff Flowers

GLACIER PARK

28 *Staff Flowers:* This view is of a flower box on an employee dormitory next to the Lake Mc-Donald Lodge. Each summer Glacier Park, Inc., hires hundreds of U.S. and foreign college students and retired folks to work in the hotels and stores in the park. These people need places to stay and to serve them there are dorms and cabins, such as this one, located around the hotel complexes.

I thought that this view would be a nice change of pace from the grand mountain scenes that populate this book. There is a simple beauty to the scene—the brightly colored, irregularly shaped flowers against the dull brown, geometric siding of the building.

One day, when I was visiting The Glacier National Park. Fund, a non-profit organization that supports the park in a big way, I brought along this piece of art. One of the staff there swooned over the piece. She told me that she immediately knew the scene as she had worked at Lake McDonald Lodge as a college student and had stayed in that very dorm. Her eyes looking upward into past memories, she told me about the housemother there who, every evening, would go to the lodge and play cards on the lobby balcony with women who worked in the gift shop. "Oh," she said, "This does bring back the memories." Maybe that's what art is all about.

29 *McDonald Shore:* You won't find this location in any guidebook. That is because it is a stretch of beach near the cabin that is provided for artists-in-residence during their stay in the park. The cabin is located on the shore of Lake McDonald off a spur road about 0.25 mile south of Lake McDonald Lodge. The view suggests how easy it is in Glacier to get away from the hubbub of a packed venue like Lake McDonald Lodge to the solitude of a lovely place.

This scene deviates from the usual blue-skies-and-sunshine views of Glacier National Park during the summer. On this day the sun has not yet risen high enough over the Continental Divide to flood the McDonald Valley with the normal July deluge of sunshine. There is a bit of an overcast to go along with the shadows.

It you look carefully, you will see faint fingers of burn along the base of the far mountain, stretching up the slopes. This is the result of the huge fires that burned in the park in the summer of 2003. Although these stripes of burn detract from the pristine look of the forests, fire is part of the natural cycle of the park and should be seen and understood by visitors just as they see and appreciate the glaciers.

McDonald Shore

© 2005 Roy E Hughes • www.royehughes.com

GLACIER PARK

Lake McDonald

GLACIER PARK

30 *Lake McDonald* is around 10 miles long and over a mile wide. It stretches in a northeast to southwest direction, starting a mile or so northeast of the Lake McDonald Lodge complex and continuing all the way to Apgar. The Going-to-the-Sun Road meanders along almost the entire length of its shoreline. There are numerous turnouts from which to gaze at the majestic mountains along the north side of the lake. This scene can be viewed from several of these turnouts.

I am very fond of this piece of artwork because it is the first scene that I did of Glacier Park. Its style is very similar to some of the travel posters done of the park in the 1920s and '30s, and it looks very much like a block print in that the areas of color are large and flat and without many details. The mountains are reduced to a bare minimum, and the forested mountainside is depicted in a single swath of color. Some of the later works that I've done have more detail and intricacy. I like that variety in my work, and I've found as I do these various scenes that the scene itself drives the way that it will turn out—whether it is more colorful or lower key, whether there is more detail or less, whether it looks more like a silkscreen print or an impressionistic painting. I like the way the scenes speak to me and tell me how to express them.

31 *Apgar Boats:* In the early 1890s, nearly twenty years before Glacier became a park, Milo Apgar homesteaded this area. Early on he recognized the tourist potential of the area and built its first cabins. Today Apgar, on Lake McDonald, is a collection of shops with a motel, restaurant, and visitor center thrown in. It is still somewhat like it was before Glacier National Park came to be.

The beach is a popular place for folks to sunbathe and dip into the glacial water. Boaters and canoeists ply the lake in nice weather. The Glacier Park Boat Company rents canoes and boats for those who don't want to trailer theirs to the park.

Spectacular mountains backdrop the north side of Lake McDonald. If you have strong binoculars you can see the Highline Trail high up on the mountains as it approaches Granite Park.

Apgar Boats

© 2005 Roy E Hughes - www.royhughes.com

GLACIER PARK

32 *Bear Country:* This is a sign that appears at the West Glacier entrance to the park. However, this view could be seen several places in the park—except for the grizz behind the sign—as these warnings are posted at every entrance.

Although this view is rather whimsical, the sign is deadly serious and carries an important message. There are a number of species of animals in Glacier that can be dangerous to humans, the grizzly bear being the most obvious. Moose, mountain lions, and other animals may, at rare times, be inclined to attack humans. However, even "more tame looking" animals, such as mountain goats and bighorn sheep, can intentionally or unintentionally injure people. Keeping a distance between people and animals is good for both.

Additionally, animals that are fed human food can become food conditioned to this type of feed and may either become dependent upon it or become pests in seeking it. Human food may not suit the digestive processes of these animals.

33 *Belton Station* is located at West Glacier, which used to be called Belton. Driving west from Marias Pass, the station is on the right side of U.S. 2, the road that runs from East Glacier to West Glacier along the southern boundary of the park.

Belton existed before the park became a park in 1910. About the time Glacier was created, the Great Northern Railway built the Belton Chalets across the road from the station. With the creation of the park, the station became a busy tourist terminal and remained so for decades as folks headed out for Apgar and Lake McDonald from here. However, with the completion of Going-to-the-Sun Road and increased reliability of automobiles, traffic through the station waned.

Today, Amtrak's Empire Builder, running between Chicago and Seattle, stops at the station daily. Freight trains rumble by frequently, their echoes joining those trains of long past who delivered throngs of tourists here. Visitors in automobiles cruise past the station looking for the north turnoff into the park, often without noticing this historic building.

Belton Amtrak

BELTON

© 2005 Roy E Hughes - www.royehughes.com

GLACIER PARK

CHAPTER 2. Many Glacier Area

Many Glacier, located in the northeast section of Glacier National Park, is the park's second most visited area, after the Going-to-the-Sun Road corridor. Head 7.5 miles west from the town of Babb, driving through Blackfeet cattle range to the park entrance station. A few miles beyond the entrance station lies the Many Glacier complex situated along the shores of Swiftcurrent Lake. The Swiftcurrent area north of the lake contains a campground, motel, store, and restaurant. The Many Glacier Hotel, on the east shore of the lake, is the largest of the park's hotels and the anchor for this area.

There are boat rides available on Swiftcurrent Lake and Lake Josephine. The hiking out of this area is spectacular with the highlights being Iceberg Lake to the north and the Grinnell Glacier trail to the south. For those less inclined, there are parking turnouts around the area that provide idyllic settings for just sitting back and enjoying the scenery and wildlife. There are often mountain goats, black bears, and grizzlies within view of these areas.

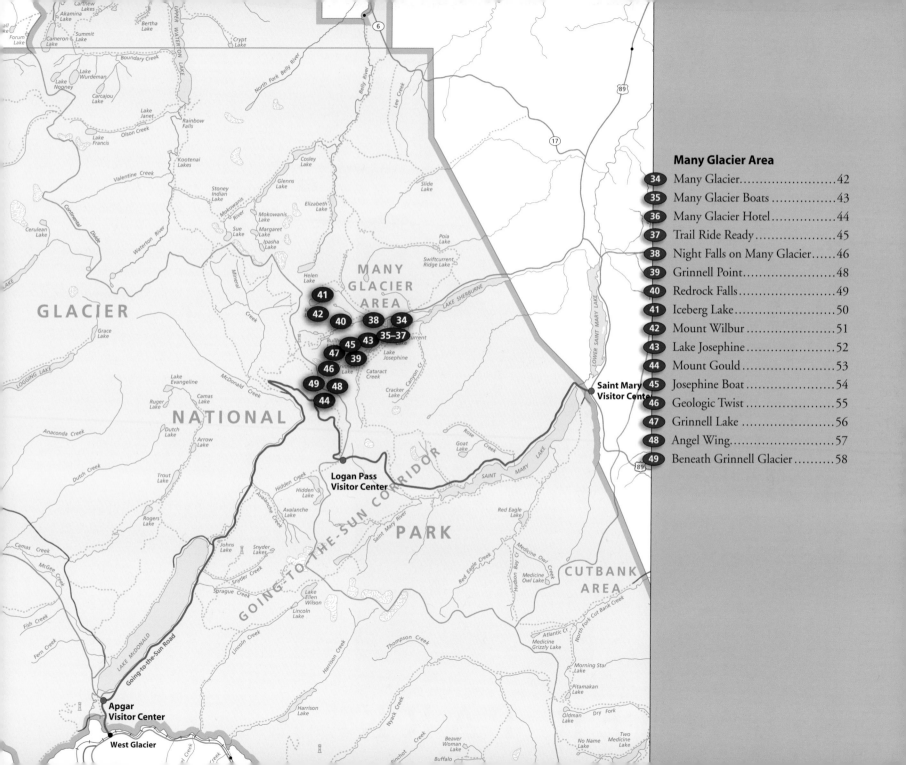

Many Glacier Area

Many Glacier

GLACIER PARK

34 *Many Glacier:* This is the first "real" view of the Many Glacier area. Although the road in from Babb has beautiful vistas, it isn't until you turn left at the Swiftcurrent complex junction and drive south toward the hotel that you feel you have arrived at Many Glacier. The view here is from the bridge over the outlet of Swiftcurrent Lake. Many Glacier Hotel can be seen in the far left. Grinnell Point is the large mountain to the right and Mount Gould and Angel Wing are in the distance. These landmarks have their own separate views later in the chapter.

In the early days of the park, visitors arrived at East Glacier (then called Midvale) by train, then suffered through a rugged two-day journey by horse-drawn coach to reach the Swiftcurrent area. By 1915 James J. Hill of the Great Northern railroad had completed the Many Glacier Hotel.

© 2005 Roy E Hughes - www.royehughes.com

Many Glacier Boats

35 *Many Glacier Boats:* A canoe and boat rental dock is located behind the Many Glacier Hotel on the lakeshore. You can rent boats, kayaks, and canoes at the heavily visited lakes in the park. Boaters should be aware that the park's tall mountains can generate harsh and sudden weather. The long, narrow configuration of the lakes allows the wind to sweep from one end to the other, changing the water from calm to white-capped waves in a short time. Boaters are advised to stay close to shore.

Some sightseers prefer the powerboat tour of the lake instead. In the larger craft, tourists can view the scenery from the comfort of an enclosed cabin.

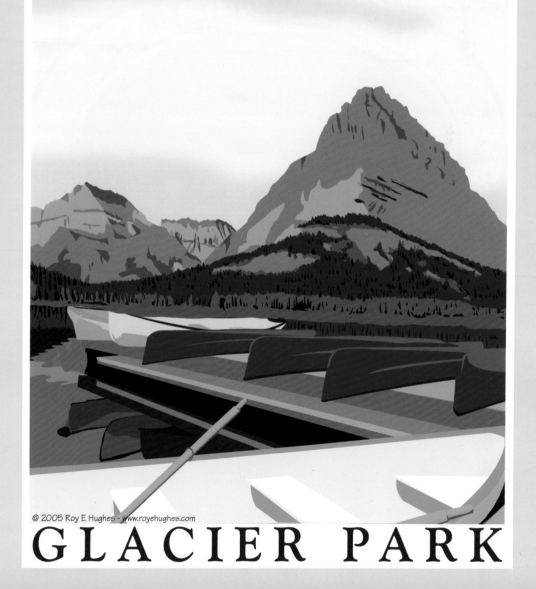

© 2005 Roy E Hughes - www.royehughes.com

GLACIER PARK

MANY GLACIER HOTEL

GLACIER NATIONAL PARK

36 *Many Glacier Hotel:* You can see a distant view of this hotel in the previous scene. You will see more views of it later in this chapter as it serves as the focal point of the Many Glacier complex.

Louis Hill, the Great Northern Railway magnate, orchestrated the construction of this huge building, which was completed in 1915. There are several good sources for learning more about this grand undertaking. A good starting place is *Architecture in the Parks: National Historic Landmark Theme Study* by Laura Soulliére Harrison.

The building's design has a Swiss chalet quality to it. It is constructed of stone and timber, including huge lobby uprights made from tree trunks hauled from the Pacific Northwest on railcars. Over the years, weather and the impact of hundreds of thousands of tourists took its toll on the building and substantial money was put into a restoration effort that is still underway.

This view, from the parking lot which is situated on a hill behind and overlooking the hotel, is framed in the design of a baggage label that was used by the railroad in the park's early days. They placed these labels on tourists' suitcases as a form of subtle advertising.

37 *Trail Ride Ready:* In the early days of Glacier National Park, horseback riding was the preferred means of transportation. The alternative was to travel by foot as there were no roads to speak of and lake travel was not common. A number of tent camps were laid out a day's ride from each other along the trails so that after a day of riding and viewing the beautiful scenery, tourists could camp in comfort, with "lodging" and meals provided.

Today a concessioner operates the horseback rides in Glacier. This scene is at Many Glacier, where one can take half-day or daylong rides to Grinnell Lake, Cracker Lake, and other destinations. Trail rides in the Apgar area are shorter and geared more to novice riders. From the Lake McDonald complex one can do a short forest ride or climb from the lake high into the mountains to Sperry Chalet, as a day ride or for an overnight stay.

Trail Ride Ready

© 2008 Roy E Hughes - royehughes.com

GLACIER PARK

38 *Night Falls on Many Glacier:* Here we see the hotel from a parking area across Swiftcurrent Lake after sunset. This parking area, offering picnic facilities, a restroom, trailheads, and glorious views all around, is just off the road that leads to the Swiftcurrent buildings north and west of the lake.

From this vantage point one can see how this large hotel rises several stories high along the shore. At this distance, however, it is difficult to see the intricate "Swiss jigsaw" moldings around the windows and balconies lining the west façade, or the fire escapes that are cleverly integrated into the balconies. It is a beautiful and imposing building.

During the winter the hotel is closed and snow often piles and drifts high around the building. A caretaker spends the winter shoveling snow off the roof and checking the deserted and ghostly interior, floor by floor and room by room, to make sure that no damage has occurred from the weather. The hotel is frigid and inhospitable during this harsh season, and the caretaker resides in a nearby cabin equipped with electricity, satellite TV, and Internet access. Loneliness with comfort.

Grinnell Point

GLACIER PARK

39 *Grinnell Point:* George Bird Grinnell's name is attached to a number of features in the Many Glacier area, including Grinnell Glacier and Grinnell Point. Grinnell was a hunter, scout, and guide in the late 1800s who became a strong advocate for the creation of Glacier National Park. Many historians of the park consider him to be the "father" of Glacier. A historian, naturalist, and writer, he also published *Forest and Stream* magazine. The story of his life and his efforts to create the park make interesting reading. *Grinnell's Glacier* by Gerald Diettert is a good place to begin learning.

Grinnell Point was originally known as Stark Peak, after Pearly Stark, "an early day miner who had a claim on the side of the mountain," according to Donald Robertson in *Through the Years in Glacier National Park.* It is located on the west side of Swiftcurrent Lake. By Glacier standards, the mountain is relatively short, topping out at about 7,600 feet. Dr. J. Gordon Edwards, in his classic *A Climber's Guide to Glacier National Park,* says, "This is an easy half-day hike from Many Glacier Hotel…" I am going to take his word for it. In the foreground of this view you can see the road to the hotel across the outlet to Swiftcurrent Lake and the beginning of Swiftcurrent Falls.

Redrock Falls

GLACIER PARK

40 *Redrock Falls:* This is a great hike to do with an interpretive ranger. Follow the ranger west past the Swiftcurrent buildings and onto the trail up the Swiftcurrent Valley leading to Fishercap Lake, Redrock Lake, and Redrock Falls. This popular route is about 3.5 easy miles roundtrip and done at a leisurely pace. The out-of-shape can catch their breath at the many stops where the ranger explains the flora, fauna, and history of the area.

These rangers are fonts of enjoyable knowledge. We learned that "Fishercap" is the American Indian name given to George Bird Grinnell.

But for a photographer, Redrock Falls is the high point. The falls actually have two levels, and it is impossible to find a location from which to see the whole falls complex at one time. Thus in this rendition I resorted to focusing on the lower falls and creating an insert in the upper right corner where I depict the upper falls. The two scenes are seen from different physical points of view along the trail.

Iceberg Lake

41 *Iceberg Lake,* in the Many Glacier area, can be accessed from the Swiftcurrent complex. The 9.5-mile roundtrip hike follows the Swiftcurrent Valley trail for a bit, then bends north. It is a long hike but doesn't feel long, perhaps due to the fantastic vistas that occupy your eyes during the trek. The lake is beautiful, nestled beneath the cliffs formed by the ridge of the Continental Divide.

GLACIER PARK

42 *Mount Wilbur* is located to the west of Swiftcurrent Lake. It is one of the many places in the park named for dead white men. In 1885, naturalist George Bird Grinnell named Mount Wilbur for E.R. Wilbur, a partner of his. The American Indians called the mountain Heavy Shield. The latter name has my personal vote.

The mountain is delightful to look at, and some find it lovely to climb. Norman Clyde pioneered the idea, and in 1923 he became the first to summit the 9,000-plus-foot peak. There are now a number of routes up Mount Wilbur. None of them appear easy.

George Ruhle, in *Roads and Trails of Waterton-Glacier International Peace Park: the Ruhle Handbook,* warns that the climb should only be attempted by experienced hikers. Ruhle goes on to tell of the Fourth of July that he and another guy climbed the peak to set off flares as a show for Many Glacier Hotel tourists. By the time they got to the top, clouds had settled in, ending what he retrospectively labeled as an "absurd stunt."

Mount Wilbur

© 2008 Roy E Hughes - www.royehughes.com

GLACIER PARK

Lake Josephine

GLACIER PARK

43 *Lake Josephine,* the shy sister of Swiftcurrent Lake, hides behind a dividing land bridge at its south end. To reach her you either have to hike down Swiftcurrent Lake or take the cruise boat from the Many Glacier Hotel to the lake's south end, disembark, and walk a few hundred feet south through the woods. Here there is another boat dock and another tour boat that will take you on a cruise of Lake Josephine and either drop you at the southern dock or bring you back to the northern landing. This scene shows an early-morning boat running south on the lake, before the sun has risen to dispel the shadows.

Lake Josephine is a paternoster lake, as are Swiftcurrent and Grinnell Lakes, located further up this U-shaped valley carved out by a glacier. Those of the Catholic faith likely know that paternoster's Latin origin, *pater noster,* translates as "our father." When applied to physical objects, paternoster refers to things in a chain or loop. Since Grinnell, Josephine, and Swiftcurrent form a chain of lakes, one can see how the term is applied to them.

44 *Mount Gould:* The Continental Divide runs through Glacier Park. A portion of this stretch of mountains is called the Garden Wall. Mount Gould is situated on this "wall." At a height of over 9,500 feet, the peak can be seen from the west side of the park, but it's more dramatic viewed from the east side as shown in this image.

This dominating peak appears in a number of scenes in my artwork. Here the view is from the tour boat plying its way south on Lake Josephine in the Many Glacier area. A closer view of the mountain can be had from the Grinnell Glacier Trail, which climbs from Lake Josephine.

People have been climbing the easier west side of Mount Gould since 1920. However, the east side was not climbed until 1965. "This [route] is only for expert mountaineers who are equipped with ropes and pitons and proficient in their use," advises J. Gordon Edwards, the late guru of Glacier climbers, in his 1995 edition of *A Climber's Guide to Glacier National Park.*

Mount Gould

© 2007 Roy E Hughes - www.royehughes.com

GLACIER PARK

Josephine Boat

GLACIER PARK

© 2007 Roy E Hughes · www.royehughes.com

45 *Josephine Boat:* Lake Josephine almost attaches to Swiftcurrent Lake at Many Glacier, and the Glacier Park Boat Company provides a tour of both lakes. You'll begin aboard the boat *Chief Two Guns.* When you reach the south end of Swiftcurrent Lake, take a short walk across the land that divides the two lakes and board the *Morning Eagle* for a tour of Lake Josephine.

A boat tour on the lake is an excellent way to see wildlife. More than once grizzly bears have been encountered on the walk between the lakes. Moose are often seen near the lakeshore. You can also watch hikers wending their way along the north shore on the Grinnell Glacier trail. If you wish, you can depart the boat at the south end of the lake and take a later boat back. Or you can hike several miles back to the hotel.

The large mountain in the background of this view is Mount Gould. Angel Wing tucks beneath its right side.

Geologic Twist

46 *Geologic Twist:* Glacier National Park is a geology buff's treasure trove. This scene is found along the Grinnell Glacier trail. You can see how rock layers have been folded and twisted into an amazing portrait of nature's power.

In the Proterozoic era, 1,600 to 800 million years ago, huge bodies of water covered the area, forming sedimentary rocks like those shown here. Then, 170 million years ago, the Lewis Overthrust occurred, creating the mountains that make up Glacier Park. During the last ice age, glaciers carved away much of those mountains, exposing many of the geologic features that you can see today. Once dominant, these glaciers are now rapidly disappearing.

GLACIER PARK

Grinnell Lake

© 2006 Roy E Hughes - www.royehughes.com

GLACIER PARK

47 *Grinnell Lake,* located about a mile up the valley above Lake Josephine in the Many Glacier area, is yet another park landmark named after renowned naturalist George Bird Grinnell. The backdrop of this lake is more famous than the lake itself. Mount Gould and its shoulder, Angel Wing, form the huge massif seen behind the lake. As with many lakes in glacier country, Grinnell has that enchanting aquamarine color resulting from "glacial dust" in the water reflecting light.

In 1912 Morton Elrod wrote a booklet entitled *Some Lakes of Glacier National Park.* He and his party found that the lake was "well supplied with microscopic life." Elrod mentions that the "lower end of the lake is open and park-like, but marshy. . . . It is possible to ride out into the water a distance of a hundred feet or more before the water reaches the horse's belly."

It is likely that Elrod was the last person who conducted this experiment. Today, even though there is a trail to the lake, most people opt for the more rigorous and scenic hike to Grinnell Glacier. This view depicted here is from the Grinnell Glacier trail.

48 *Angel Wing:* You can see in the image where this hunk of rock on the shoulder of Mount Gould gets its shape. I added some artistic touches to make the "wing" a little more obvious. Most references to Angel Wing are in terms of passing by it or where it is in relation to Mount Gould, which gets all the attention, being bigger and brassier. But you would be hard pressed to find a more heavenly name than Angel Wing, and there should be more about this mountain. There should be a story about nuns making a pilgrimage to the site. Or there should be a tale of a lover throwing himself off the peak for unrequited love. However, there is no dramatic history for the place.

Local character Jim Egan did climb up there via the Grinnell Glacier trail in 1997 with George Ostrom and the Over The Hill Gang—you can learn more about them in the book *Glacier's Secrets.* The "gang" is a group of hikers, mostly in their 60s and 70s, who do weekly hikes in the park during the summer. Jim has climbed over 187 peaks in Glacier. So, although there is no dramatic history to be found for Angel Wing, folks like Jim and the gang don't mind. They just like the view from the top.

49 *Beneath Grinnell Glacier:* First of all, the Grinnell Glacier trail doesn't go all the way to Grinnell Glacier. In 1924 when Morton J. Elrod published the first *Elrod's Guide & Book of Information,* the trail went as far as it does today, but it did go to the glacier. How can that be?

The reason for this is that the formal trail ends today at a picnic area below a mass of glacial detritus that at one time was part of the glacier itself. It is a huffer of a climb from the picnic area up and over this talus to reach Upper Grinnell Lake, which used to be glacial ice instead of water. Thus, where the foot of the glacier ended in Elrod's day is now a picnic area.

Grinnell Glacier, at the foot of the cliffs, is a mere ice cube of its former self. At one time the small, elongated glacier on the cliffs to the right, called the Salamander, was joined with it. In fact, Grinnell Glacier once covered the entire area beyond the green foreground in this view.

CHAPTER 3. Two Medicine Area

In the southeast corner of the park—and outside the park—lie the Two Medicine area and the town of East Glacier, once called Midvale. Although East Glacier and the Glacier Park Hotel get their share of visitors arriving via U.S. Highway 2, the Two Medicine area is not as heavily traveled as other areas of the park. There are good hiking trails there, but no accommodations outside the East Glacier area.

During the 1890s James J. Hill, the empire-builder owner of the Great Northern Railway, extended his railroad from Minneapolis toward the west coast. Marias Pass, the U.S. 2 corridor south of the park, proved the best route for crossing the Rocky Mountains. Midvale was situated at the east entry to the pass, and eventually the Glacier Park Station for the Great Northern Railway was located there.

After Glacier became a park, Hill and his son Louis began building roads and tourist accommodations to lure railroad passengers there. The Hills were instrumental in developing tourist draws in the park.

East Glacier is actually outside the park on the Blackfeet Reservation. The Two Medicine area is reached by driving 6 miles north on Highway 49 toward St. Mary, then turning west to enter the park after a short distance. The road continues for a few miles to the Two Medicine store and campground area, where it ends.

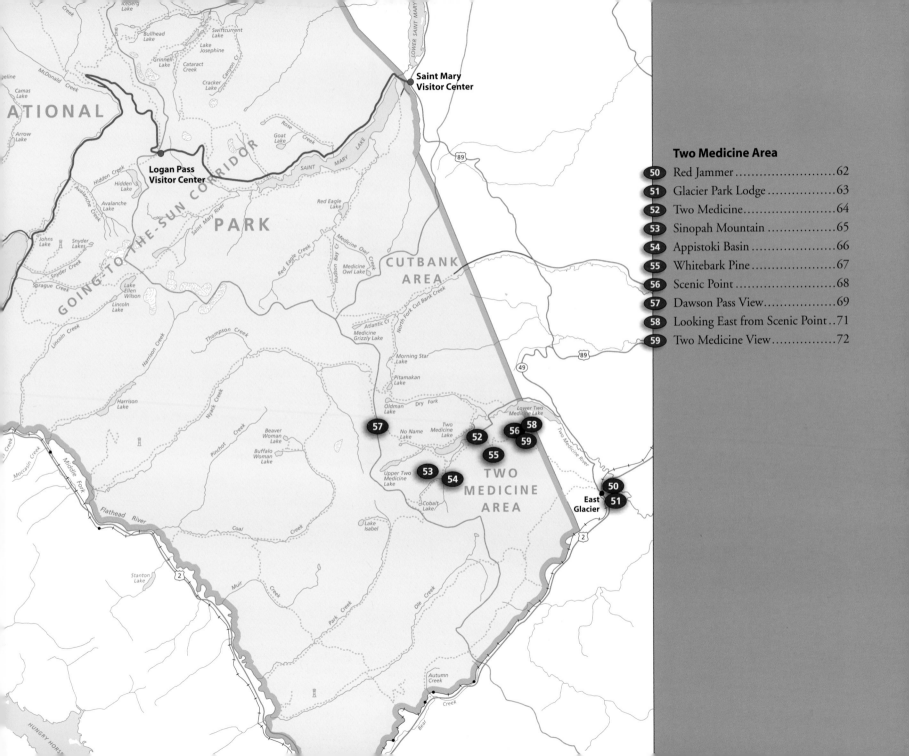

Two Medicine Area

Red Jammer

GLACIER PARK

50 *Red Jammer:* This red bus, a familiar sight plying the roads of Glacier Park, is shown in front of the Glacier Park Lodge in East Glacier. From the early days of the park, when automobiles were as primitive as the roads upon which they traveled, touring cars and buses carried hardy tourists to the area's remote reaches. In the 1930s the White Motor Company provided the park with buses such as the one depicted. These were used until they began to wear out and parts were no longer available. In 1999 the buses stopped running due to safety concerns.

Ford Motor Company stepped up in 2000 and restored each of the thirty-three buses by removing its body and setting it onto a modified E-450 truck chassis powered by a propane-burning V8 engine. Other features were restored or modified to enhance safety as well, and in eighteen months the fleet was back on the road.

These buses are often called "jammers" due to the balky gearshift mechanism of the original manual transmissions. However, drivers of these buses are quick to tell you that the driver was the jammer, the one who had to do the shifting by jamming the gears. With the automatic transmissions in the restored vehicles, the argument becomes moot.

51 *Glacier Park Lodge* is in the town of East Glacier, and is not actually in Glacier National Park but within the neighboring Blackfeet Indian Reservation. East Glacier lies on U.S. Highway 2. The Great Northern Railway line coming from Chicago once passed by here.

The railway actually built this hotel, as well as other tourist accommodations in the park, to lure people to Glacier via the railroad. The Great Northern Railway formed the Glacier Park Hotel Company, which began building these accommodations in 1911.

This massive log and timber building was patterned after the Lewis and Clark Centennial Exposition's Forestry Building, which was built in 1905 in Portland, Oregon. You can see in the image the massive intricacy of the lobby structure. It is fitted with period furniture, the balcony is ringed with huge oil paintings, and design detail is evident in the lights that hang from high over-head. The huge tree trunks were shipped in on railroad cars from the Pacific Northwest. The detail in this scene presented me with the artistic challenge of getting everything right. I spent over eighty hours developing this interior view.

Glacier Park Lodge

© 2007 Roy E Hughes - www.royehughes.com

GLACIER PARK

Two Medicine

GLACIER PARK

52 *The Two Medicine* entrance to the park is a few miles north of the town of East Glacier at the end of Lower Two Medicine Lake. There are three "Two Medicine" lakes. At Two Medicine Lake you'll find the Two Medicine Store, shown here, a campground, and a trail system. This area isn't as heavily trafficked as the Going-to-the-Sun corridor or Many Glacier, but the Scenic Point hike and the Dawson–Pitamakan loop are very popular. You'll also find a trail leading to Upper Two Medicine Lake.

In 1934 when President Franklin Roosevelt visited here, this building was known as the Two Medicine Chalet. During his visit, the President was inducted into the Blackfeet tribe at this location.

The mountain seen behind the building is Rising Wolf. It is named for a white man, Hugh Monroe. He was the first white man to live with the Blackfeet and tended to arise from sleeping by pushing himself up from a crawling position, thus he was called Rising Wolf.

Sinopah Mountain

© 2007 Roy E Hughes · www.royehughes.com

GLACIER PARK

53 *Sinopah Mountain* rises from Two Medicine Lake, at the head of the valley. It is a handsome mountain, sometimes reflected in still waters and sometimes fragmented in the wind-tossed lake.

What does the name Sinopah mean? It depends on whom you ask. "Fox woman" and "kit fox" are two interpretations. It is agreed upon that the mountain was named for the Blackfeet wife of Hugh Monroe, mentioned in the previous view. This woman was also the daughter of a powerful Blackfeet chief named Lone Walker.

In geologic terms, 8,271-foot Sinopah Mountain is a horn. A horn is a steep mountain peak created by several glaciers carving different sides of the same mountain. There are a number of examples of horns found in Glacier.

Appistoki Basin

GLACIER PARK

54 *Appistoki Basin:* On the trail to Scenic Point in the Two Medicine country, one meanders up the shoulder of a hillside, looking at this basin in the distance. Actually there may not officially be an Appistoki Basin, but an Interpretive Ranger said that's likely what it's called, and I couldn't find anyone to tell me otherwise, so that's what I'm calling it. It's a bewitching place, especially when the sun plays hide and seek behind the bulbous summer clouds that often roll across the skies in this country. At these times the landscape is almost melodic with the rhythms of light and shadow as they race across the countryside, now bright, now dark. It is like watching a cosmic kaleidoscope in action, yet the effect is surprisingly tranquil. You are fortunate if you can experience this area at a time like this.

55 *Whitebark Pine:* This tree is located on the Scenic Point trail in the Two Medicine area. It is dead and barkless and bleached white, a beautiful filigree of twisted branches.

The pine is a "keystone" species to Glacier, meaning that it is an essential food source for many birds and animals in the park. It has seed cones that are harvested by various animals. The nuts in the cones are later eaten and passed and new trees evolve from these recycled seeds.

Since 1910, however, these trees have been attacked by a fungus called white pine blister rust. Scientists have found no effective way of stopping the spread of the disease, and slowly many of the whitebark pines, and other pine species in the park, are succumbing to this scourge.

In his great book *Glacier's Secrets: Beyond the Roads and Above the Clouds,* George Ostrom says that a ranger told him that these trees were called "silent dog trees" because the have no bark.

Whitebark Pine

GLACIER PARK

Scenic Point

GLACIER PARK

56 *Scenic Point* is viewed here from near the Two Medicine entrance to Glacier Park. Scenic Point looks like just any other mountain. It is the view from Scenic Point, that makes it notable.

57 *Dawson Pass View:* The easiest way to reach this fabulous view is to take the boat from the Two Medicine store complex to the end of the lake, then begin the hike. Otherwise, you'll add an additional 3.3 miles (one-way) of hiking onto your trek. From the boat dock it is about 0.25 mile to the Two Medicine–Dawson Pass trail and 3.4 miles and a climb of 2,450 feet from there to the pass. Fit and enthusiastic hikers can make a 15-plus-mile loop of this hike, proceeding from the pass on to Pitamakan and back to the Two Medicine campground.

Much of the hike climbs through the woods, and the trail doesn't break into the wide open for great views until a half mile or so from the top. This view from the pass looks west toward some of the most remote southern areas of the park.

Although the last bit of climb to the pass is a huffer, it is pleasant enough. There is usually a breeze blowing down from the pass, which often turns into a near gale near the top. There are tales of folks setting their packs down only to see them kite off into the far reaches. With winds sometimes reaching 40 or 50 miles per hour, it is best to batten down the hatches—and hats, cameras, jackets, and packs.

In this view, the pass is doused in sunlight while ominous clouds hang over the far mountains, giving credence once more to the adage that the mountains in Glacier create their own weather. This scene is of a sunny August day. The next day it snowed several inches here.

Dawson Pass View

© 2008 Roy E Hughes · www.royehughes.com

GLACIER PARK

58 *Looking East from Scenic Point:*
This mountain is located in the Two Medicine area; to reach its summit, begin at the trailhead located off the Two Medicine road. You'll hike 3.1 miles and gain 2,242 feet in elevation. The hike is assigned a difficulty rating of moderately strenuous. On a hot day in the summer, the mileage and elevation gain seem like more, and the difficulty rating seems a bit conservative.

Nonetheless, the trail provides wonderful scenery and a view worth the effort. Looking out to the east across the plains, it seems that if you squint hard enough, you will be able to see Chicago on the horizon. Flat, flat, flat. Turn the other direction and you have views of Two Medicine Lake and mountains ranging away into the distance. A meeting of two worlds.

If you take the ranger-led hike, the ranger will instruct members of your party to spread out as you reach the flat summit and take individual routes to the edge of the tabletop to avoid grinding trails into the tender vegetation there.

59 *Two Medicine Viewed from Scenic Point:* This happy hiker is reposing atop Scenic Point in the Two Medicine area, having hiked up the rather strenuous trail. He is gazing off to the west across Two Medicine Lake at the mountains that go on and on. The mountain in the right panel is Rising Wolf. In the left panel is Sinopah.

A *New York Times* reporter described this area as "a landscape of jumbled, snow-capped peaks, valleys bisected by frothing rivers and basins embracing alpine lakes whose water [is] as blue as that of the Caribbean." No wonder this hiker is happy.

CHAPTER 4. North Fork of the Flathead River Area

The North Fork is as much a state of mind as it is a geographical area. The folks up here like their peace and quiet—to the extent that they don't want the road paved, they don't want the potholes fixed, and they don't want power lines.

The North Fork Road runs north from Columbia Falls to the Canadian border. You used to be able to pass the U.S. immigration portal and bounce into Canada, stopping at their rustic immigration office. However, this border crossing was closed after September 11.

Only about two percent of the two million people visiting Glacier Park in a year come to this scenic northwest corner; the other ninety-eight percent are making a mistake. Besides the yummy baked goods at the Polebridge Mercantile and great dinners at the Northern Lights Saloon, the scenery around Bowman and Kintla Lakes and Big Prairie are too good to miss.

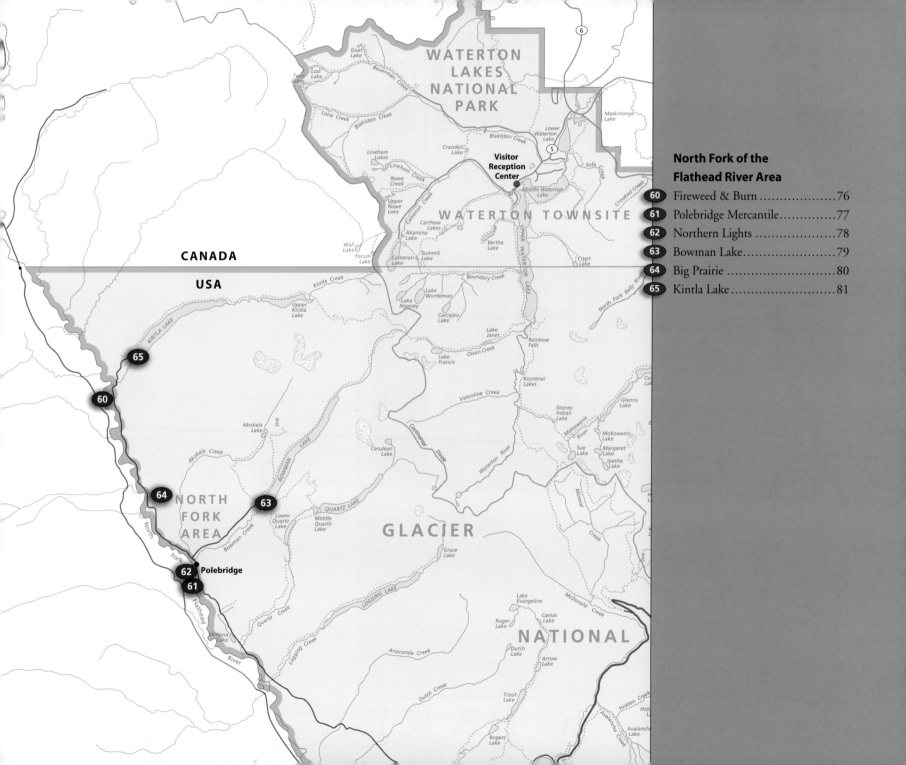

WATERTON
LAKES
NATIONAL
PARK

WATERTON TOWNSITE

Visitor
Reception
Center

CANADA

USA

**North Fork of the
Flathead River Area**

NORTH
FORK
AREA

Polebridge

GLACIER

NATIONAL

Fireweed & Burn

© 2005 Roy E. Hughes - www.royehughes.com

GLACIER PARK

60 *Fireweed & Burn:* You can see similar scenes many places in Glacier National Park, but this particular one is from along the North Fork Road, which parallels the North Fork of the Flathead River, a few miles north of Polebridge. There is a park entrance not far from here, but this area is not heavily frequented by the typical tourist.

The blackened trees in this view are lodgepole pines, charred by a forest fire. The colorful pink flowers at the foot of the trees are fireweed, named because they are among the first plants to rejuvenate after a fire. The gorgeous pink flowers, with the counterpoint of the stark, black verticals of the charred trunks, captivate visitors who happen across such a scene.

Lodgepole pines are now more prevalent in Glacier National Park than they were in the past because they have replaced other species of trees, such as cedars and hemlocks, that have perished in fires. This is because one way these pines reproduce is via what are called "serotonous seed cones"— cones that are opened by the high temperature of fire, allowing them to release their seeds.

Fireweed also flourishes after a fire, quickly populating recently burned areas. According to author and naturalist David Rockwell, "Fireweed, the seeds of which are carried by the tens of millions on the wind, blankets the entire burn in the following summer, and then turns it to a mallow pink."

61 *Polebridge Mercantile:* Mystical Polebridge lies up the rough North Fork Road from Columbia Falls. Once there was a pole bridge here across the North Fork, however, in 1988 a fire destroyed the pole bridge and it was replaced by a concrete span. The old name remains. "Concretebridge" just doesn't have the cachet.

There are other things to see and do up this direction, but the "Merc" is the magnet. This building was built in 1914 by Bill Adair and added to the National Register of Historic Places in 1986. Anybody who visits the place adds it to their personal register of fantastic places the moment they step inside.

Although the natives rely on the Merc for basic staples, visitors drool over the lip-smacking good pastry items, baked daily by the owner. The Merc hasn't changed a whole lot in nearly a hundred years, and people like it that way.

Polebridge Mercantile

POLEBRIDGE MERCANTILE

BAKERY

© 2005 Roy E Hughes - www.royehughes.com

GLACIER PARK

Northern Lights

© 2005 Roy E Hughes - www.royehughes.com

GLACIER PARK

62 *Northern Lights:* Next door to the Polebridge Mercantile, up the North Fork Road on the west side of Glacier Park, is the Northern Lights Saloon. Yes!

Folks who've been there—and most of them have been there frequently—will tell you that this scene without cars parked in front and without the porch and front lawn teeming with people is very unusual. Must be that the Northern Lights is closed, because when it's open it's usually jammed.

There aren't many places up the North Fork where a thirsty traveler can get a cool drink such as a gin and tonic or a pint of Moose Drool. And then there is the food. Who would have thought that it would be possible to get a gourmet-type meal in the wilds of the North Fork? Although the menu is limited, the food is grand. Friday night is pizza night, with three pie options: red, meat, or green.

Of course, adding to all that is the charm of the friendly feeling log and wood interior with intricate carving on the woodwork and a draped canvas ceiling. Tables are shared among parties, as is the conversation. This is a place that draws one back again and again.

Bowman Lake

© 2005 Roy E Hughes - www.royehughes.com

GLACIER PARK

63 *Bowman Lake:* There are four large lakes in the northwest corner of Glacier Park: Logging, Quartz, Bowman, and Kintla. You have to hike into Logging Lake and Quartz Lakes, but you can drive to Bowman and Kintla Lakes. The short, bumpy, dirt-road drive to Bowman Lake from the Polebridge entrance cuts through burned-over lodgepole forest, but it seems like a super highway compared to the road to Kintla Lake.

On one trip to Bowman Lake, I noticed that the road was littered with a half dozen or so unmatched shoes scattered in and along the road. Although the road is rough, that did not explain the shoes. On other trips no shoes were evident. Strange.

At Bowman Lake you'll find a campground, ranger cabin, and tranquility. This environment is for sitting and enjoying the beauty or taking off on a hike, perhaps to the Numa Ridge Lookout, about 12 miles out and back, overlooking the lake on the north side.

Big Prairie

GLACIER PARK

64 *Big Prairie:* Most of the visitors to Glacier National Park don't wander further up the North Fork than Polebridge. By not entering the park at the Polebridge entrance they miss a glorious bit of what appears to be the Great Plains transplanted to northwest Montana.

This relatively treeless area in a land of forests contains sagebrush, unusual for this area. The pretty yellow flowers in the picture are leafy spurge. The name doesn't sound as pretty as the plant looks, but it matches its nasty nature. Leafy spurge is regarded as one of the most threatening weeds in the park. This non-native species squeezes out natives and threatens to take over the area. Park employees are attempting to control its spread. In this apparently heavenly setting, a widespread prairie with a glorious mountain backdrop, it is shocking to realize that the beauty is threatened by a mere weed.

65 *Kintla Lake:* The Glacier Park website calls this the most remote "frontcountry" campground. I'd call it the most backcountry frontcountry campground. Drive north from the Polebridge entrance past Big Prairie and Round Prairie and over the roughest, bumpiest, jounciest road that you've ever taken and you'll arrive at the Kintla Lake Campground—and Kintla Lake. The road is only 14 miles long, but it feels like 100.

The last time that I was at Kintla Lake, I mentioned to Ranger Lyle, who has been a summer fixture at the lake for approaching two decades, that I thought the road was not quite as rough this year. He reported that after a new superintendent had traveled the road on a familiarization tour he directed some funds and a grader towards it as he found it unacceptably rough. Lyle said that something happened partway along and the grader was reassigned.

In this image, a canoe awaits paddlers for an idyllic cruise on this placid lake. Don't be fooled, however, as sudden winds can raise menacing waves in a few minutes. Rangers instruct boaters to stay close to shore. Still, each year a number of boaters find themselves spilled into the frigid waters. Drowning is the number one cause of death in the park. Be careful.

Kintla Lake

GLACIER PARK

CHAPTER 5. Backcountry

Ah, the backcountry. Where is it exactly? In Glacier National Park, what is commonly referred to as backcountry begins about 100 yards from any road or building. Yet the majority of travelers do not experience any of Glacier's backcountry. What a shame.

Although the backcountry can be accessed from any road in the park, this chapter focuses on the backcountry north of Logan Pass along the Continental Divide, then extending down into Many Glacier. Also included is the backcountry south of Lake McDonald, up toward Sperry Glacier. These are highlights. An entire book could be dedicated to artwork of beautiful views throughout the million acres of the park. For now, these will have to suffice.

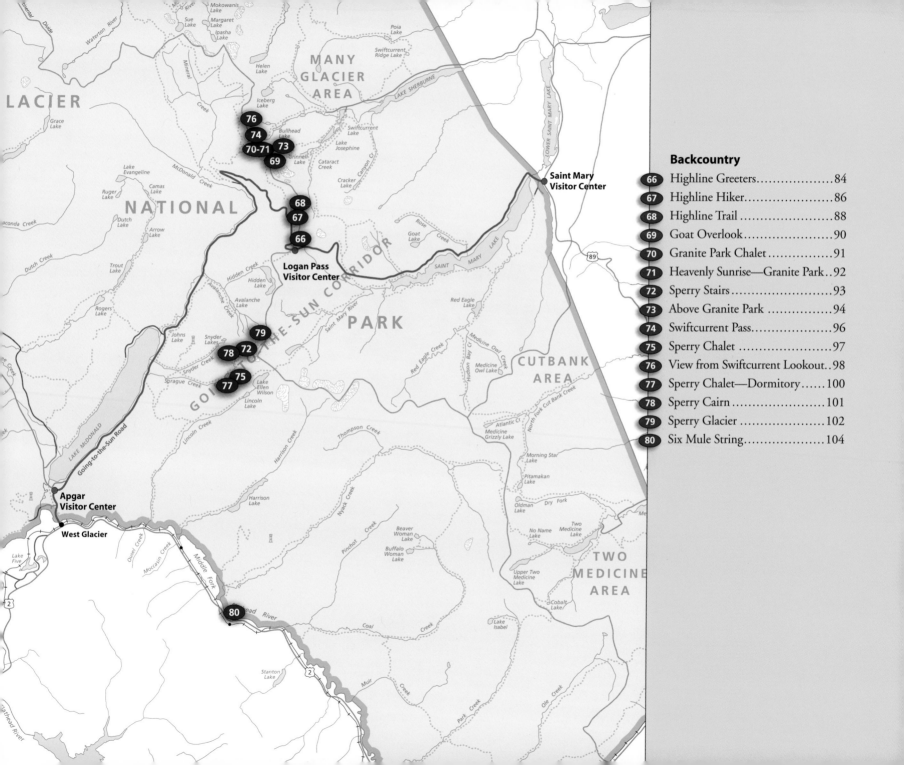

66 *Highline Greeters:* Many hikers think that the Highline Trail is the most scenic in the park. Though there are some that rival and perhaps surpass it in vistas, none of them are so accessible to so many people. Starting from the north side of Logan Pass, the trail winds 30 miles along the Continental Divide to Goat Haunt at the south end of Waterton Lake.

To travel to Goat Haunt, it is necessary to secure permits for backcountry camping along the way. These must be reserved months in advance and are often difficult to secure. However, many hikers content themselves with hiking out and back a few miles, or walking the 11-mile loop to Granite Park Chalet, then down to The Loop on the Going-to-the-Sun Road, where they can catch a free shuttle back to the pass.

This scene shows a family of mountain goats that frequent the area. They appear to be waiting to greet hikers passing by on the trail while watching the traffic far below on the Going-to-the-Sun Road. Farther along, two hikers have stopped to peer cautiously over the edge to the road several hundred feet below.

This 0.25-mile stretch of trail a few hundred yards beyond the Logan Pass start is not for those who fear "exposure," which is hiker-talk for sharp drop-offs. There is a hose-covered cable attached to the wall on the inside of the trail if you feel the need to grab on to something.

67 *Highline Hiker:* This view is a few miles north of Logan Pass on the Highline Trail. The time is late morning and the sun has highlighted Heavens Peak and other mountains out across the McDonald Valley, but the Garden Wall shades the west side of the Continental Divide.

The woman in this image is hiking to Granite Park Chalet to stay the night. Although park policy recommends not hiking alone in Glacier, she is by herself. However, hiking the Highline in mid-summer at mid-day is not really hiking alone as there are many people on the trail at that time. Yes, it's possible to find yourself alone on a stretch of trail for some minutes, but usually you are not far from other hikers.

68 *Highline Trail:* At about 3.5 miles, this trail north of Logan Pass ends the gentle up and down of the traverse below The Garden Wall and begins to switchback up the side of Haystack Butte. It is a bit of a huffer up to a saddle.

Often mountain goats frequent the foot of the switchbacks, and ground squirrels inhabit the saddle area. Because of views like the one illustrated here, not to mention the exertion of the climb, many hikers choose to stop at the saddle for lunch or a snack. That may be the reason for so many little critters darting in and out of the rocks.

If hikers are not diligent in protecting their foodstuffs, they may find them missing. A friend of mine lost a good chunk of sandwich to a marauding ground squirrel while he was admiring the gorgeous view. Park visitors are not supposed to feed the animals, but the animals don't know that.

The trail climbs a bit beyond the saddle, as shown, then levels off for a while before resuming fairly gentle rises and falls between here and Granite Park.

Goat Overlook

© 2005 Roy E Hughes · www.royehughes.c

GLACIER PARK

69 *Goat Overlook:* With Granite Park Chalet in sight 0.5-mile away, a trail junction provides an opportunity to climb a side trail to the Grinnell Glacier Overlook. It's only a bit over 0.75 mile to reach the Continental Divide and a glorious view down into the Swiftcurrent Valley. However, the trail is steep and the distance seems longer, especially on a hot summer afternoon.

The climb is definitely worth the effort. From the top one can look hundreds of feet straight down to Grinnell Glacier, then follow the valley down past Grinnell Lake, Lake Josephine, Swiftcurrent Lake, Lake Sherburne and out to the plains beyond. Adventurous visitors can follow a goat trail 0.25 mile or so south to reach a gap in the rock that provides an even better view. Be advised that this area is subject to healthy winds that can possibly throw a person off balance.

Granite Park Chalet

G L A C I E R P A R K

70 *Granite Park Chalet* can be reached by several hiking trails. The most popular approach is along the Highline Trail from Logan Pass, a distance of about 7.5 miles. From The Loop on the Going-to-the-Sun Road, it's a 4-mile climb to reach the chalet. A third longer and more strenuous route starts at the Swiftcurrent complex and climbs up and over Swiftcurrent Pass, then drops to the Chalet.

It should be explained that this view of Granite Park Chalet cannot be seen by mere mortals. The point of view here is from thin air about a hundred yards west of the buildings. Cliffs drop off a few feet in front of the main chalet building, so I had to create this view from combining a number of photographs and applying some architectural drafting techniques.

Granite Park Chalet is a not-full-service chalet, meaning that hikers need to pack in their food and bedding. An industrial strength kitchen is available for use, and freeze-dried food may be purchased at the chalet. Bedding may also be rented. This and Sperry Chalet are often fully booked before the trails are clear of snow. If you want a spot, plan ahead and book early.

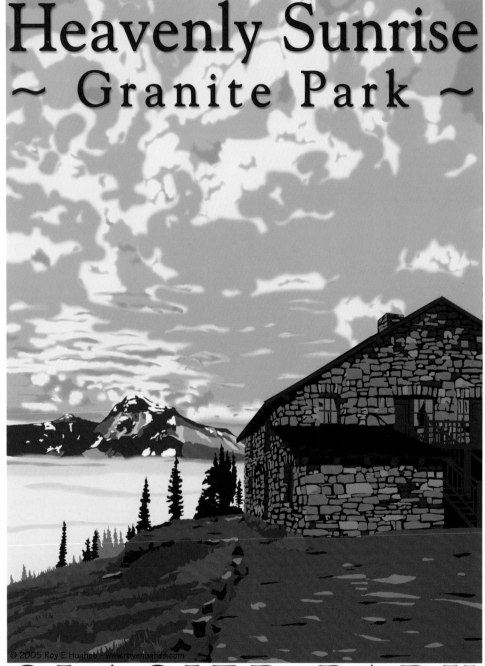

Heavenly Sunrise
~ Granite Park ~

© 2005 Roy E Hughes · www.royehughes.com

GLACIER PARK

71 *Heavenly Sunrise—Granite Park:* Ray Djuff and Chris Morrison tell the full story of the park chalets in their wonderful book *Glacier's Historic Hotels & Chalets.* Suffice it to say that Granite Park Chalet was built in 1914–15 by the Great Northern Railway. The buildings were made of local stone because of the lack of available timber. Ironically, there is no granite in Glacier National Park.

In the early days of the park, travel by horseback was the means of transportation in the high country, and a series of chalets and tent camps was built throughout the park. Having hiked some of these precipitous trails, I can attest to the fact that I would not have wanted to ride a horse along them.

This view is of a morning after a storm, with oblique rays of the sun creating a heavenly lighting effect. Heavens Peak, in the distance, is lit with a golden glow as the clouds filling the McDonald Valley to a level of over 6,000 feet appear as an iridescent sea of white. In the foreground is the dining hall main building of the chalet complex.

If heaven exists, it must be like this.

Sperry Stairs

GLACIER PARK

72 *Sperry Stairs:* On the Sperry Glacier trail, there is a cliff on the east end of a glacier-formed shelf marked with cairns and tarns. Once, access to Comeau Pass above the cliffs could only be gained by climbing the cliff. Later, a steel ladder made the pass more accessible. Still, many of the early tourists who ventured up to Sperry Glacier were not fond of the idea of ascending the 90-foot-high ladder. About 1930, a set of stairs was built into a gap, called a chimney, in the face of the cliff. The stairway is steep and narrow, and the stairs are rough and vary in height and tread width. To help hikers ascend and descend this route, a steel cable has been strung through eyebolts driven into the rock sides, forming a crude handrail.

There is a story, which sounds a lot like a folk tale, about a hiker climbing the stairs who ran into a grizzly bear descending the passage. According to the story, the bear squeezed by the hiker and both continued on their journeys unscathed. Having climbed up and down this narrow stairway, I tend to doubt that a person and grizzly bear could pass by each other, even on good terms.

73 *Above Granite Park:* From Granite Park Chalet, one can hike north along the northern Highline Trail clear to Waterton Lake on the Canadian border, down to The Loop on the Going-to-the-Sun Road, back south along the Highline Trail to Logan Pass, or up eastward toward Swiftcurrent Pass. This view is from the Swiftcurrent Pass trail, looking west across McDonald Valley toward Heavens Peak in the distance. Lake McDonald lies hidden in the valley behind the mountain in the left foreground. Visible in the view is the main chalet building containing the dining hall on the first floor and guest rooms on the second. The roof of the sleeping dormitory is seen behind the trees in the foreground. Close inspection will reveal part of the ranger quarters between the two buildings.

To the far left of the chalet area are the composting outhouses. In 1992 the chalet was closed, in part, due to poor sanitation facilities. A citizens' effort resulted in funds being raised to restore this and Sperry Chalet, including the addition of up-to-date toilet facilities. Visitors must still bring their own drinking water, however, or draw it from a spring 0.25 mile away.

Swiftcurrent Pass

GLACIER PARK

74 *Swiftcurrent Pass* sits on the Continental Divide between the Highline Trail and the Swiftcurrent Trail at an elevation of 7,185 feet. The cairn indicates the summit of the pass.

This view is artistically contrived, as it is not possible to see into Swiftcurrent Valley from the pass. You have to actually walk about 0.5 mile east to see into the valley.

Once, I hiked to the pass with a buddy after an overnight in Granite Park Chalet. During the previous night's evening program, we had heard from an employee that grizzlies habituated the area, but that black bears did not come up this high. A quarter mile east of the pass's summit, we stopped on the trail so my friend could attend to his camera. As I stood waiting I detected a movement to my right about 6 feet south of the trail. I turned to see a young, cinnamon colored black bear sauntering by on his way toward the valley. As I remember, I nodded a hello to him and he, looking at me, nodded back. He continued on his way and I suggested to my friend that he look behind him. He did and jumped just a bit.

People behind us said that the bear had followed us all the way up and over the pass from Granite Park. I am very glad that the bear was a peaceable fellow. I had no time to think of camera or bear spray before he was far down the trail.

Sperry Chalet

GLACIER PARK

© 2005 Roy E Hughes - www.royehughes.com

75 *Sperry Chalet* is 6.4 miles and a 3,400-foot climb above the Lake McDonald complex. The trail to reach the chalets belies the destination itself. There are no views to speak of and in the heat of summer it is dusty and oppressing. You can walk the trail, or for a change of pace, cover it on horseback.

The hike is worth it to reach Sperry Chalet, as the artwork suggests. This view had to be created from photos shot from various angles, as the point of view is a spot in mid-air a hundred yards in front of the structures. Sperry is a full service facility, offering not only lodging but food as well, including a great breakfast, a trail lunch, and a revolving menu of three dinners. From here, you can trek on up to Sperry Glacier or up and over Gunsight Pass and down to Going-to-the-Sun Road at the Jackson Glacier Overlook.

In 1911 and 1912, tourists here stayed in tents, but by 1914 Italian stonemasons had completed the dining hall and the guest dormitory, nowadays called the "hotel." As with Granite Park Chalet, the facility was closed for a while in the 1990s while a state-of-the-art composting toilet facility was constructed.

76 *View from Swiftcurrent Lookout:*
If you think the climb is over when you've reached the top of Swiftcurrent Pass, think again if you plan to visit Swiftcurrent Lookout. The trail to the lookout branches off to the north just west of the pass and grinds 1.4 torturous miles with nearly 1,300 feet elevation gain up switchbacks to the lookout and magnificent views all around. This is the highest point in Glacier that you can get to by a maintained trail.

When you've reached the lookout, you've reached the summit of Swiftcurrent Mountain at an elevation of 8,436 feet. Above the treeline here, the mountain is mostly screefields and low plants: forbs (non-woody, broad-leaved plants), lichen, and some shrub cover.

The fire lookout here was built of stone with a frame top structure in 1935 and staffed until 1990. The park began staffing the lookout again in 2001 after refurbishing it. This building is listed on the National Historic Lookout Register.

Sperry Chalet
~ Dormitory ~

© 2005 Roy E Hughes - www.royehughes.com

GLACIER PARK

77 *Sperry Chalet—Dormitory:* This view is from the west end of the guest dormitory, or hotel. Beyond the building a hundred feet or so is the toilet facility, and another couple of hundred feet beyond that is the stone dining hall. In the dark of night, with critters of all shapes and sizes flitting about, guests tend to make a quick trip between buildings, flashlights dancing like lightning bugs.

The two-floor hotel will accommodate seventy-five people. Each floor contains about a dozen rooms of varying size. The walls are paper-thin and sound transmits well. The ten o'clock "lights out" is welcome to weary travelers, especially if they have talkative neighbors.

Sharp-eyed observers can see the letters "G N Ry" in light stones worked into the gable end. This, of course, stands for Great Northern Railway. At times, guests can sit on the porch and balconies and watch mountain goats browse nonchalantly on the plants near the building.

78 *Sperry Cairn:* The trail from Sperry Chalet to Sperry Glacier is 6.8 miles roundtrip, with a 1,600-foot elevation gain. Although it is a taxing hike, the scenery is so breath-taking that the grind is eased by the views. And the variety of terrain makes the hike a most interesting one.

From the chalet, the trail glides up and around the left side of a glacier-formed valley, passing alongside of and beneath waterfalls. The cairn seen in this image is on a level spot after the long first climbing portion of the trail. It appears to be a wide and deep floor of a hanging valley. This area contains some small tarns, or ponds. This view is looking north and over the edge. Lake McDonald lies several thousand feet below. You can continue on from here to reach Sperry Glacier.

Cairn is Scottish for a pile of rocks. Scots bred dogs to go amongst cairns to kill vermin and the breed became known as Cairn Terriers. Cairns— the stone kind—are used to mark travel routes.

Sperry Cairn

GLACIER PARK

79 *Sperry Glacier:* After making it up the stairway carved into a cliff on the Sperry Glacier trail, you arrive at 8,000-foot Comeau Pass. Sperry Glacier is about another mile eastward across a glacial plain, the trail marked with cairns.

This glacier was named for Dr. Lyman Sperry, an amateur explorer who first visited this area in the late 1890s. Although George Bird Grinnell is considered by many to be the "father" of Glacier National Park, Sperry was also an early advocate for setting aside this land.

This view of Sperry Glacier is from north of the foot of the glacier. Comeau Pass is seen as the low, flat section along the skyline to the right of the image. The path from the pass to the edge of the glacier follows to the left of that point straight across the image to the glacier's edge below the snow-capped peak in the center. Most people hiking to the glacier do not see it from this perspective.

Of course, when Dr. Sperry first saw this glacier it was much larger than it is today. The Repeat Photography project on the Northern Rocky Mountain Science Center web site, www.nrmsc.usgs.gov, shows photos of the glacier taken in 1913 and 2005 that reveal the glacier has been reduced by two-thirds over that period.

80 *Six Mule String:* This scene occurred a couple of miles east of Coal Creek on U.S. Highway 2 about 15 miles east of West Glacier. It depicts a packer bringing a pack string south across the Middle Fork of the Flathead River, the park boundary on the south. The packer had been into the park taking provisions to a trail crew in the backcountry.

While horses and mules were once the only means of transportation in the area that is now Glacier Park, today there are fewer and fewer of them. There are the concession horse rides out of Many Glacier and Lake McDonald. Granite Park and Sperry Chalets are supplied by pack string. And the park maintains a coral and stock near the West Glacier entrance.

CHAPTER 6. Waterton Lakes National Park, Canada

You don't need to look too closely at this chapter's map to notice that something is amiss: two of the views aren't in Canada! I've chosen to include the images of both Goat Haunt and Chief Mountain here because both are views you probably would not see unless you made the trip to Waterton Lakes National Park in Canada.

You'll pass by the Belly River and Chief Mountain areas on your way to Canada. From the Many Glacier junction at Babb, follow U.S. Highway 89 north for 4 miles. Head left on the Chief Mountain International Highway to reach Waterton Lakes National Park.

Waterton Townsite is situated on Waterton Lake and one can take a tour boat south on the lake to Goat Haunt, which is inside the United States. There is a border station and campers' shelter at Goat Haunt, along with trails leading off south into the heart of Glacier Park. Winding through the mountains, one soon approaches the border and the turn off into the Belly River area, a little-visited section of the park that is mostly a destination for hikers.

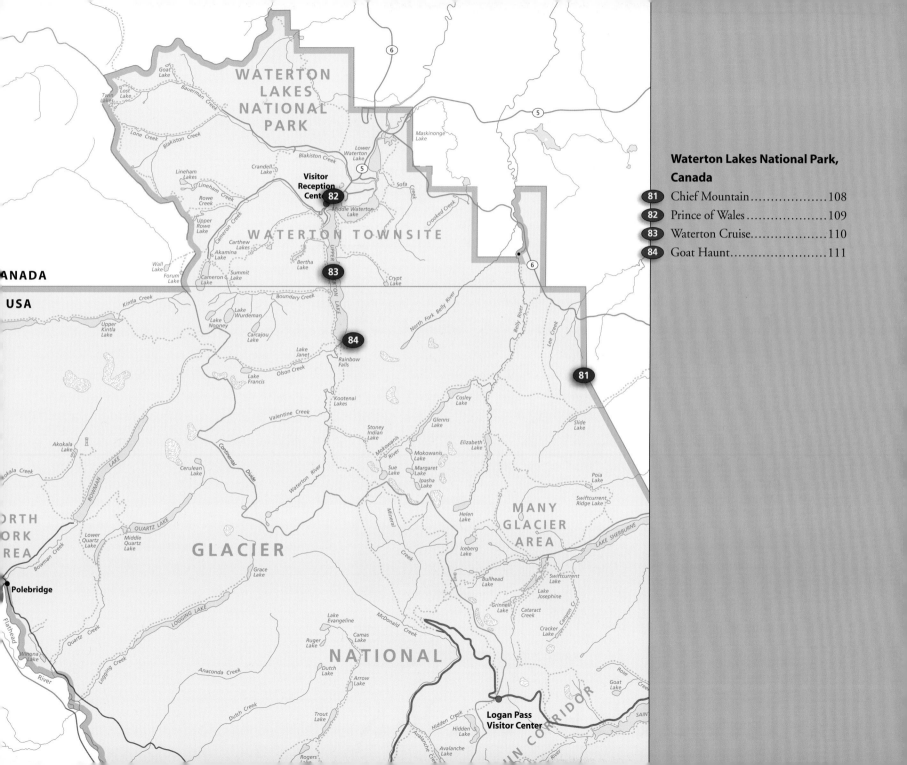

WATERTON
LAKES
NATIONAL
PARK

WATERTON TOWNSITE

Visitor Reception Centre

82

83

84

81

CANADA

USA

GLACIER

NATIONAL

NORTH FORK AREA

Polebridge

MANY GLACIER AREA

Logan Pass Visitor Center

Waterton Lakes National Park, Canada

Chief Mountain

© 2005 Roy E Hughes - www.royehughes.com

GLACIER PARK

81 *Chief Mountain:* If Glacier National Park were a theme park, this amazing mountain would be placed near the St. Mary entrance to attract tourists. However, Glacier isn't a theme park, and Chief Mountain is located north of St. Mary and the Many Glacier turn off, along the Chief Mountain International Highway that leads north to Belly River, the Canadian border, and Waterton Lakes National Park beyond. The mountain is visible for hundreds of miles from three directions.

Chief Mountain has a full history, beyond repeating here. Suffice to say that the mountain was a holy place for American Indians of various tribes, to whom it was known by a number of names, all of them having to do with "chief." There is a legend that an Indian brave long ago hauled a buffalo skull to the top of this formidable hunk of rock to conduct a vision quest, using the skull as a sacred pillow. Many famous people, like Lewis and Clark, viewed the mountain during their explorations.

82 *Prince of Wales:* This amazing Swiss-style hotel was completed in 1926 as part of the accommodations scheme for Glacier and Waterton parks. Louis Hill of the Great Northern Railway, who was responsible for having the hotels in Glacier constructed, wanted to build the hotel in 1913, but World War I interfered with this idea.

In *Glacier's Historic Hotels and Chalets: View with a Room,* Ray Djuff and Chris Morrison chronicle the problems of attempting to build a huge hotel in the wilds of Waterton. From a base at Cardston, 30 miles away, the contractors had to haul materials across seas of mud and drifts of snow. The result was worth the effort.

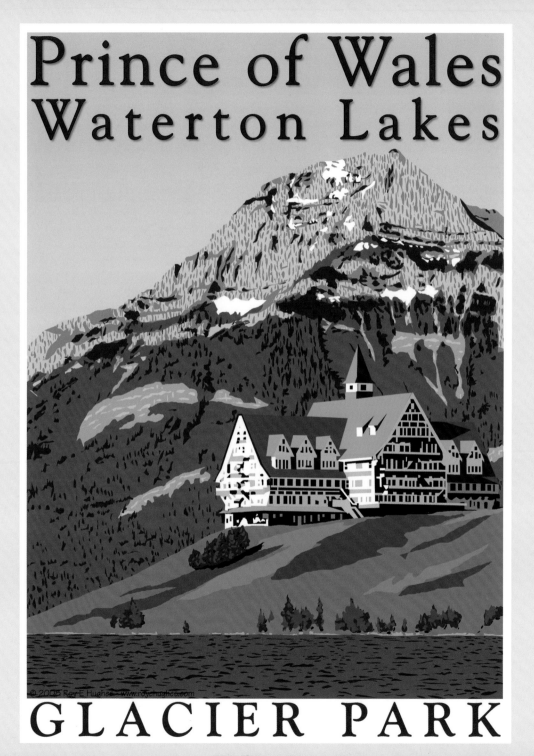

Waterton Cruise

GLACIER PARK

© 2008 Roy E Hunt

83 *Waterton Cruise:* Waterton Lake runs about 11 kilometers—remember that we are in Canada now—or 7 miles south from Waterton townsite to Goat Haunt at the southern end of the lake. Goat Haunt is in the United States, so this is an international cruise. And what better name for the tour boat that plies these waters than the *M. V. International?*

For over two hours, you can lean on the rails of the boat and gawk at the splendid scenery while listening to the captain's running commentary. If there is wildlife about the shore, the captain and crew will likely know about it and swing as near as is legal so that passengers can take photos.

At Goat Haunt there is an exhibit pavilion and U.S. immigration—you are returning to the United States, so have your identification ready. Most people spend a half hour walking about the area, then re-board the boat for the return trip to Waterton townsite. Intrepid hikers may shoulder their packs and start south for Logan Pass, 31 miles away.

84 *Goat Haunt:* Although one can hike 13.8 kilometers (8.7 miles) down the east side of Waterton Lake to reach Goat Haunt, most folks take the boat to get there. There is an exhibit pavilion here and a U.S. immigration point. A valid passport is required for entry.

For a while after September 11, this border crossing was closed to prevent terrorists from entering the U.S. at this point. It took until May of 2003 for the border to be reopened.

Goat Haunt

© 2008 Roy E Hughes - www.royehughes.com

GLACIER PARK

CHAPTER 7. Cut Bank Area

Between Two Medicine, to the south, and the eastern entrance to the park at St. Mary, lies the Cut Bank area. This remote section of the park is accessed by several miles of dirt road and offers regal scenery and a rather primitive campground.

In the days before the park was created, Native Americans used this portal to cross the mountains from east to west. Later, in the early days of the park, there was a teepee camp there for tourists that included a dining hall. Eighteen cabins were built to form the Cut Bank Chalets. Most people traveling to Cut Bank in the early days either hiked in or rode horses. This area was more visited during that time than it is now.

Due to the increased popularity and availability of automobile travel, as well as the economic problems of the Depression, the chalets ceased being used in 1933. Lying dormant through World War II, they deteriorated to the point that they were torn down in 1948. Today the Cut Bank area is a quiet, little-visited area of the Park.

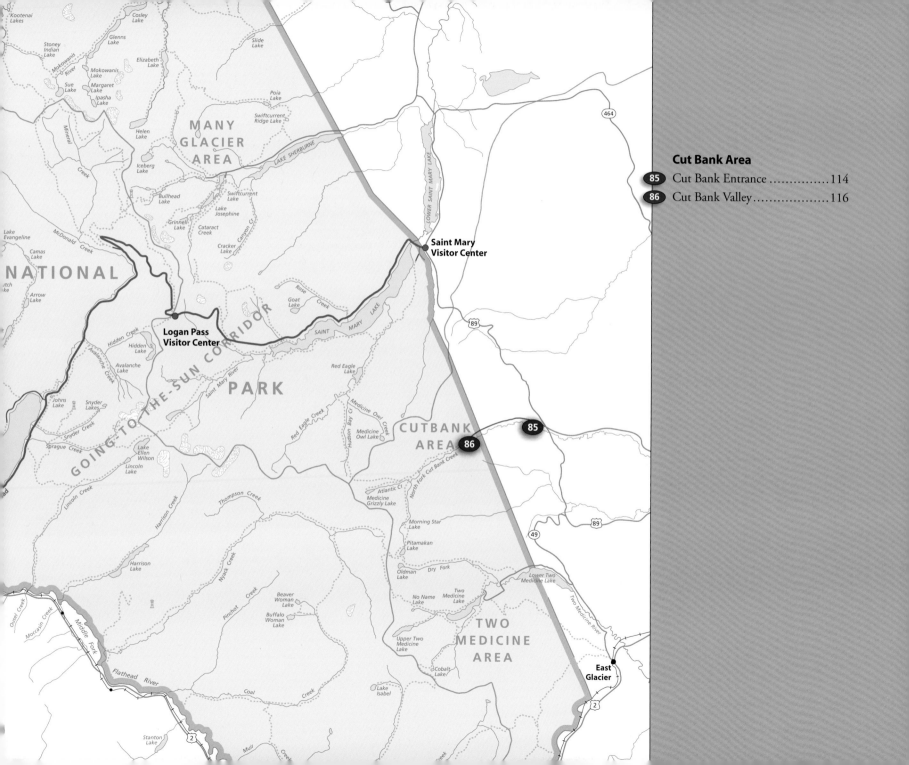

85 *Cut Bank Entrance* doesn't feature any fancy-schmancy stone welcoming signs, just a brown and white metal sign hanging from a pole. It is a 5-mile ride over a sometimes-bumpy road to reach Cut Bank proper, which consists of a ranger residence and a primitive campground where there is no water available. You think that you are driving down a ranch road and wonder if you might be on the wrong road—but you aren't.

This view shows some of the mountains to the west from the entrance. Some of these mountains are named for, or by, white men and some have American Indian names. You can figure out which is which: Mad Wolf, Eagle Plume, Stimson, Razoredge or Running Fox, and James.

86 *Cut Bank Valley* is far less traveled than the other areas of the park. In 2007 over two million people visited Glacier National Park. Of those, only twelve thousand visited Cut Bank. As the park web site says, "Cut Bank offers campers the opportunity to enjoy a primitive camping experience with serenity and solitude." Most people who come here don't lounge around the campground; they head off into the backcountry on one of the many trails that radiate from here.

CHAPTER 8. Animals of Glacier National Park

The gorgeous scenery is the reason that most people come to Glacier National Park. But some of them, I'm sure, would trade all that lovely landscape for one good sighting of a prime grizzly bear. For aficionados of fauna, Glacier is a potential paradise. There are animals of all kinds in all parts of the park. However, the trick is in being at the right place at the right time to see them.

Some are easy to see. The deer, both white-tail and mule, are downright common. Elk can often be seen in the meadow areas between St. Mary and Rising Sun. Black bears often cause traffic jams along Going-to-the-Sun Road. Logan Pass is a good place to look for mountain goats and bighorn sheep. In the Many Glacier area it is not unusual to spot a grizzly from the road. Moose can sometimes be seen from the road as well.

Other animals are either more rare or more difficult to see. Mountain lions frequent the North Fork area but are seldom seen. Some gray wolves live in the same area and are just as elusive. Bobcats, lynx, and wolverines are also rarely spotted. Still, the fun is in the looking.

My artwork is based on reference photos, most of which I take myself. I occasionally rely on public domain photos. Some of my views are closely related to the reference photos, some hardly resemble the photos at all, and some views are constructed from photo composites. Some of the wildlife scenes here are based on photos drawn from the Glacier National Park, U.S. Fish & Wildlife Service, and Yellowstone National Park websites. I am grateful that these resources are available.

Grizzly Bear

© 2008 Roy E. Hughes · www.royehughes.com

GLACIER PARK

87 *Grizzly Bear:* The most prized view in Glacier National Park is likely the grizzly bear, although you don't want to see one close up. People have long been infatuated with grizzlies, and there are facts, stories, lore, and myths surrounding this magnificent beast.

It should be pointed out that the black bear and grizzly bear can look very similar, especially in the brush and at a distance. Black bears come in a variety of colors and sizes, as do grizzlies. The grizzly has a distinctive hump above its front shoulders; however, in certain postures the black bear can appear to have a hump as well.

Probably the best area of the park in which to safely observe grizzlies is the Many Glacier area. During the summer months, grizzlies—often sows with cubs—browse the slopes on the north side of the road between the turnoff to the Many Glacier Hotel and the Swiftcurrent complex.

Visitors are cautioned about bears as they enter the park, and rangers continually remind them that bears can be unpredictable. Take these warnings seriously, and don't risk your life and the life of the bear to get "that perfect picture."

88 *Black Bear:* This bear was spotted just off the road at The Loop on the Going-to-the-Sun Road. It is a black black bear. Black bears are often not black; they can be brown, cinnamon, or blond.

Black bears are very common in Glacier. They generally tend to mind their business and often don't appear to be perturbed with the presence of people. However, it is important for visitors to learn about bear's behavior so they can make appropriate decisions when encountering them.

In the "old" days people were allowed to feed animals from their cars, and the bears became quite attracted to human food. This was bad for the bears because once they become food conditioned to human food they become more of a potential danger. Today feeding any animal in the park is prohibited, for the sake of both the animal and the tourists.

Black Bear

© 2005 Roy E Hughes - www.royehughes.com

GLACIER PARK

Mountain Goats

GLACIER PARK

© 2008 Roy E Hughes - www.royehughes.com

89 *Mountain Goats* can appear to be some of the most beatific animals. With dark limpid eyes poised above the long slender slope of white face that ends in a coal black nose, the goat possesses a tranquil look while browsing or at rest. Long white hair covers the mountain goat's compact, chunky body, exposing only the goat's eyes, nose, hooves, and short, black, curved horns. Both billies and nannies have horns.

The docile look of this animal does not suggest its amazing agility on steep, rocky terrain. To watch these goats leap off a near vertical rock face and bound safely down several hundred feet is amazing. Their hooves have hard outer edges and soft "sticky" centers. Their legs act as shock absorbers as they land on the rock after a leap.

Visitors to Glacier are fortunate in that they can readily see mountain goats in many locations. The area around Logan Pass Visitor Center is a convenient area from which to observe these delightful animals—at a safe distance.

90 *Bighorn Sheep* carry horns that can be described as massive. They range from six to thirteen inches long. An expert observer can determine the age of a ram by the amount of curled horn that he possesses. Ewe bighorns have smaller, lighter horns. Bighorns are brownish in color, with lighter underparts. Although they can move rapidly, most people in Glacier Park see them ambling along mountain slopes or grazing contentedly. They feed on grasses and other plants during the summer and on bunchgrass and shrubs in the winter. During mating season the rams compete for the ewes by bashing their huge horns against each other. Those who have witnessed this ritual say that the sound can be heard for a long distance.

Bighorn Sheep

GLACIER PARK

Bull Moose

© 2006 Roy E Hughes - www.royehughes.com

GLACIER PARK

91 *Bull Moose:* So, which would you rather run into in the brush, a grizzly bear or a bull moose? The correct response is: neither. However, for all the notoriety that the grizz gets, the moose deserves just as much respect.

Moose can be seen throughout the park area, although they seem to prefer the Many Glacier area. Only once did I see one too close for comfort. I rounded a bend in the trail and saw a large bull a hundred feet or so off the trail peacefully browsing on evergreen boughs. He looked at me and I looked at him, then I gently backed up around the corner and waited until he was finished dining and had moved on before I continued on the trail.

Although moose appear to be tranquil critters most of the time, I have heard of a bull that took the grill and radiator off the front of a two-ton truck that was trying to nudge him off the road. Bull moose are the largest antlered animals in the world. They can weigh up to twelve hundred pounds. Their huge forequarters and massive antlers make them appear to weigh every bit that much.

92 *Mule Deer Pair:* Look at the ears on these poor dears, and tell me where the mule deer gets its name. Delightful to look at, these deer are found all over Glacier Park and way beyond. They are sometimes confused with the white-tail deer.

Mule deer are often seen early in the morning and in the evening, as those times coincide with their daily meal times. They will eat grass and shrubs and other green plants and aren't adverse to a good hay field. Population problems sometimes occur in protected areas such as the park when the deer become too numerous for the environment to support them.

As fun as it is to watch mule deer pose, it is as delightful to watch them run. These graceful creatures run in bounds, leaping high and long and landing lightly, only to leap again. They keep their feet together while doing this, looking as if they have pogo sticks built into them.

Whitetail Fawn

GLACIER PARK

93 *Whitetail Fawn:* Who can resist a baby deer? These little guys are usually born as singles the first time a doe gives birth and twins thereafter. Their variegated coat and white spots help keep them camouflaged in the foliage for protection from predators. Mamas teach the babies to keep absolutely still unless instructed to move. It is possible to almost step on a hiding fawn if its mother runs off to draw potential danger to her and away from her baby. By the end of summer, this little fawn will have lost its white spots and be a leggy little thing that more closely resembles mommy or daddy.

Bucks shed their antlers each year in the winter and grow new antlers back in the spring. As the antlers grow, they become covered with velvet, which the deer then rub off on trees before the mating season in the fall. The size of a buck's antlers is related to age and nutrition.

Whitetailed deer tend to be more nocturnal than mule deer. They are also more secretive and solitary than the social mule deer. However, like the mule deer, whitetails eat grass and shrubs, as well as fruits and berries.

94 *Majestic Elk:* "Majestic" is a word that comes readily to mind when viewing an elk with an impressive rack of antlers. There is a hugeness and beauty and grace to these animals.

You will often see a number of elk together, as they tend to be herd animals. In summer older cow elk will usually lead a herd of cows, calves, and yearling bulls. During breeding season in the fall, bull elk will congregate a harem and challenge other bulls for dominance by bugling. Cows produce a single calf in May or June, unlike deer, which may bear twins. Like deer, elk eat grasses and shrubs and also young trees.

In early morning during the summer, it is not unusual to see a number of cars parked by the side of the road between St. Mary and Rising Sun, and the meadow to the north of the road populated by tourists with long-lensed cameras mounted on tripods. A hundred or so yards north, near the trees, there is often a herd of elk patiently standing or browsing to the clicks of shutters.

Majestic Elk

© 2008 Roy E. Hughes · www.royehughes.com

GLACIER PARK

Mountain Lion

GLACIER PARK

© 2008 Roy E Hughes - www.royehughes.com

95 *Mountain Lion:* You will likely never see a mountain lion posed like this. In fact, you will be lucky if you ever see a mountain lion at all in Glacier National Park. Oh, there are many of them about; quite a few reside in the North Fork area. However, these catamounts, cougars, painters, panthers, pumas, or screamers—take your choice of name—are usually quiet, unseen denizens of the forest.

I have seen one up the North Fork and this image does not do the beast justice. The mountain lion I saw was crosswise in the road and seemed to stretch clear across it. From the tip of his nose to the tip of his tail he was a lengthy critter. These cats range in length from 6 to 8 feet. Some can be even larger. They appear long and lean and graceful and nothing to mess with.

Occasionally these animals will attack humans, especially children, however, their main fare is deer, elk, an occasional moose, and assorted small animals, such as rabbits. Somehow mountain lions also eat porcupines.

Coyote in Winter

© 2008 Roy E Hughes - www.royehughes.com

GLACIER PARK

96 *Coyote in Winter:* When living in the wilds, coyotes will eat just about anything, plants or animals. They will eat animals and birds found dead or alive. They will eat various types of fruit. They will eat grasshoppers and crickets. They will even take on a deer or elk under the right conditions.

In the places where their territory intersects with ours, coyotes often get a bum rap for this indiscriminate appetite. In cities and suburban areas, they sometimes turn to cats and dogs to eat, making them unpopular with pet owners. In rural areas, farmers don't like coyotes because they will eat chickens and sheep if they can. Few folks would list the coyote among their favorite animals.

Still, there is a grace associated with the coyote, unless it appears in an emaciated condition, that is a little like that of a wolf or fox. "Wily" is a term that has been applied to this animal. Many American Indian tribes have the coyote in their tales, often as a trickster.

Gray Wolf Winter

© 2008 Roy E Hughes - www.royehughes.com

GLACIER PARK

97 *Gray Wolf in Winter:* "Grandma, what big teeth you have," said Little Red Riding Hood. Since the time of Little Red wolves have had a public relations problem. Throughout Montana, and most of the West, they were pretty well wiped out in the 1900s. Farmers and ranchers don't much like them because they kill stock. However, environmental-minded folks have made efforts to bring them back. "In 1980, the Northern Rocky Mountain Wolf Recovery Team completed a plan which would guide wolf recovery efforts for a future wolf population in the northern Rockies…" according to the Montana Fish, Wildlife & Parks.

Canadian wolves crossed into Glacier around 1980 and the population grew to about forty-eight by the mid-1990s. There were two packs of wolves in the North Fork area in the 1990s—the North Camas Pack consisted of twelve animals and the South Camas Pack thirteen. By 2007 the number of packs was up to thirty-six in northwest Montana.

Just because wolves are back doesn't mean that you will see one; tracks maybe, a wolf probably not. They are ghostly creatures that tend to stay out of sight. The only wolf that I ever saw "in the wild" was ironically standing next to the train station at Lake Louise in Canada.

98 *Wolverine:* To learn more about this little-understood animal, the National Park Service funded a grant to study them in Glacier in 2002. They captured and "radio-marked" over twenty of these critters and have been able to track their movements using Global Positioning System (GPS) technology.

If you take the ranger-led hike to Redrock Falls in the Many Glacier area, the ranger may show you the catch pen where wolverines were trapped to await their radio. When a wolverine was captured, the researchers would contact a veterinarian in Kalispell who would drive to the Many Glacier gate, ski to the site, and surgically implant the radio device in the animal's abdomen.

Wolverines are about 3 feet in length and, as you can see, are not the most beautiful of animals. They will eat most anything, from roots to moose, if they can find an injured one. They live at higher elevations in summer and drop down to lower lands during the winter.

Wolverine Alert

© 2008 Roy E Hughes - www.royehughes.com

GLACIER PARK

© 2005 Roy E Hughes - www.royehughes.com

99 *River Otter* can grow to be 4 feet long, but close to half that length is tail. The otter's powerful tail and webbed feet make for a swift-swimming creature, on top of or under the water. In addition, its fur insulates it from the cold. This swimmer can stay underwater for several minutes and dive to great depths.

You don't see these animals often, as they tend to be nocturnal in summer and most people don't visit Glacier during the winter. Otter like to live in swift water with undercuts in the banks. Slower waters can serve as places for raising young. These sleek and playful critters are a treat to watch streaking through the water and sliding down slopes into a stream if one is lucky enough to catch them unaware in the wild.

River otters, technically called northern river otters, feed on fish. They will also eat frogs.

100 *Columbian Ground Squirrel:* There is a plethora of squirrel species around. A number of them are ground squirrels, including the prairie dog and the Columbian ground squirrel. The Columbian is larger than most ground squirrels; it is about a foot long and weighs about a pound.

In Glacier Park you can see them many places; Logan Pass and Lake McDonald complex to name but two. In heavily trafficked areas these animals often turn into beggars and thieves. Although feeding wild animals is prohibited in the park, many people share their potato chips and other snacks with these cute little critters.

When they are not eating human food, Columbian ground squirrels dine on grasses and bulbs. As fruit ripens they will add it to their diets as well. Occasionally they will devour an insect or two, or even a fish.

The Columbian ground squirrel has one litter a year. Outside the park these animals are often called gophers by farmers and ranchers—who do not like their digging holes in pastures where animals might trip in them.

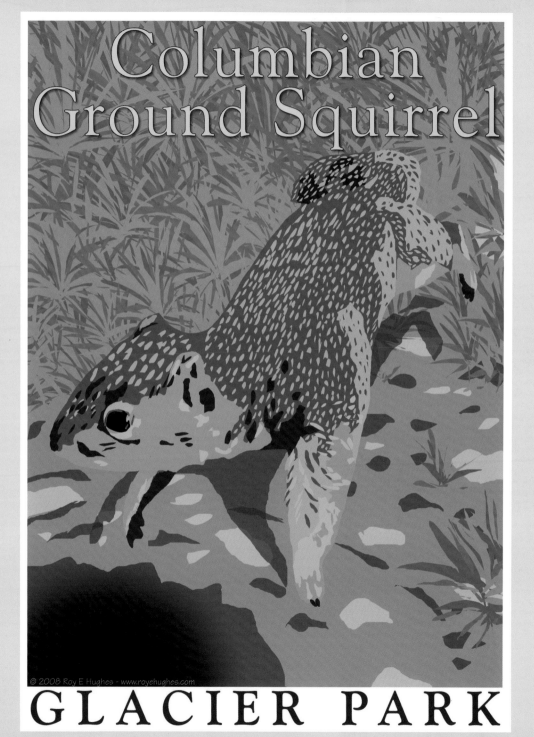

Columbian Ground Squirrel

GLACIER PARK

Further Reading

Buchholtz, C. W. *Man in Glacier.* West Glacier, MT: Glacier Natural History Association, 1976.

Diettert, Gerald A. *Grinnell's Glacier: George Bird Grinnell and Glacier National Park.* Missoula, MT: Mountain Press Publishing Company, 1992.

Djuff, Ray and Chris Morrison. *Glacier's Historic Hotels & Chalets: View with a Room.* Helena, MT: Farcountry Press, 2001.

Edwards, J. Gordon. *A Climber's Guide to Glacier National Park.* West Glacier, MT: Glacier Natural History Association, 1995.

Elrod, Morton J. *Elrod's Guide and Book of Information of Glacier National Park.* Missoula, MT: self-published, 1924.

Holterman, Jack. *Place Names of Glacier/Waterton National Parks.* West Glacier, MT: Glacier Natural History Association, 1985.

Kimball, Shannon Fitzpatrick and Peter Lesica. *Wildflowers of Glacier National Park and Surrounding Areas.* Kalispell, MT: Trillium Press, 1995.

Molvar, Erik. *Hiking Glacier and Waterton Lakes National Parks, 3rd edition.* Helena, MT: Globe Pequot Press, 2007.

Robinson, Donald H. *Through the Years in Glacier National Park.* West Glacier, MT: Glacier Natural History Association, 1960.

Schmidt, Thomas. *Glacier and Waterton Lakes National Parks and Road Guide.* Washington, D.C.: National Geographic, 2004.

Spring, Vicki. *Glacier-Waterton International Peace Park, 2nd edition.* Seattle, WA: The Mountaineers Books, 2003.

Thompson, Margaret. *High Trails of Glacier National Park.* Caldwell, ID: The Caxton Printers, Ltd., 1938.

Williams, Rebecca. *The Ruhle Handbook: Road and Trails of Waterton-Glacier International Peace Park.* West Glacier, MT: Glacier Natural History Association, 1986.